To Sheila.

So sorry to hear it
This booklet tells us
after their wives have died. Its much
harder for us than you ladies because we
are not used to domestic chores! You might
find the book a useful help!

Tony Booth.
Christmas 2016.

Without Her

ELDERLY WIDOWERS
LIVING ALONE

Edited by
JOHN I. CLARKE

The rights of John I. Clarke to be identified as the editor
of this work have been asserted in accordance with sections 77
and 78 of the Copyright Designs & Patents Act 1988.

British Library Cataloguing in Publication Data:
A catalogue record for this book is available
from the British Library.

ISBN 978-0-955031 1-4-4

Printed in Great Britain by The Coronation Press Ltd.,
Print & Copy Centre, Church Street, Coxhoe, Durham DH6 4DD

Grateful thanks to Barry Woodward
for the front cover painting.

PREFACE

This unusual little book has been written by eleven widowers all aged 75 or more who live alone in County Durham, and who wanted to express their individual feelings about losing their wives and subsequently living alone. Of course, we are not exceptional but most wives outlive their husbands, partly because they are mostly younger and partly because women have greater longevity.

Although many of us knew each other before setting out on this task, we have benefited by writing about our very different experiences and have formed a friendly group. As we felt that others who have suffered in a similar way might find our thoughts useful, we all agreed to support this publication financially and to donate any proceeds from sales to Age Concern, County Durham which has recently become part of Age UK *(see inside back cover)*.

The editor, an emeritus professor of Durham University, has been greatly helped by the varied expertise of the contributors who come from diverse walks of life and enjoy each other's company. He is also very grateful for the offer of the illustrations which embellish the book.

We all hope that many others in similar circumstances will find our efforts interesting and helpful.

CONTENTS

INTRODUCTION

Ageing and widowhood

Ageing and widowhood usually come together, but the former is a prolonged process and the latter is abrupt. With better health, less devastating wars and improved economies, populations in the developed world are ageing much more than in the past. Men in particular are living longer; not as long as women, but many are outliving their wives. Hence in an advanced country like Britain we find that there is a growing number of elderly men aged 75 or more who are widowers. Certainly not as many as elderly widows, because the ratio of women to men still increases markedly with age, so that in Britain there are three times as many women in their nineties as men.

At advanced ages, many elderly men seem to find it quite difficult to adapt to living alone. During their early married lives they became accustomed to their wives having the main domestic role, while they were the primary bread-winners. Fewer women were earners than nowadays, families were generally bigger and there were fewer marital break-ups. However, during their long lives all elderly persons have had to adjust to constant personal, social, economic and political changes. The rapidity of change is such that instead of the customary three-fold division of generations – youth, middle age and old age – there is a strong case for considering many more, as every decade brings technical and other innovations which arrive with increasing speed. For example, cars, computers and mobile phones have become almost universal household possessions in Britain, and the IT revolution dominates the lives of the young. In contrast, some of the very aged who had retired before their diffusion have opted out. Often they prefer the greater longevity and beauty of landscapes and the environment, particularly of Britain; holidays abroad were rare when they were young.

For the purpose of communication among us, there is always a danger of over-generalisation and over-classification of varied and changeable phenomena. As one becomes older, one becomes increasingly aware of the immense diversity of humankind and of individual viewpoints. For example, the varied views of elderly widower friends reflect their diverse and manifold experiences, careers and relationships. All of us see our personal situations differently, and as all views are valuable a number of them are gathered together here.

Grumpy old men

It all started with a fairly privileged, self selected group of six of us, who call ourselves 'the grumpy old men', initially two ex-doctors, three ex-academics and an ex-army officer, but when one academic died we invited a former sea captain to join us. Over the years we have gone out for regular fortnightly lunches at pub restaurants, but generally there have been no more than six of us, because several are hard-of-hearing and like to be seated at one table and involved in only one conversation. It has worked out wonderfully well, as we all have something different to offer. Some of us felt that we are surviving so successfully that we ought to put our thoughts down on paper, saying how we survived as an example to others in similar circumstances. But as not all wanted to contribute to this book, it was felt that we needed more varied views. Hence, we asked some of our other local friends if they would kindly make contributions, and thus provide a wider range of social and economic backgrounds. In the modern jargon, we became involved in social networking.

Those who provide 'personal views' in this book all live in County Durham in the North East of England, a rather distinct region with 2.6 million people and separated from the rest of England by the Scottish borders, the northern Pennines and the North York Moors. The region experiences a considerable community spirit, much more than in more southerly parts of Britain where populations have been transformed in recent decades by greater in-migration from the rest of the UK and immigration of foreigners. Some of us have spent most of our lives in the North East, influenced no doubt by professional careers and to some extent by the lower costs which enable our pensions to go further. As widowers, almost all of us also tend to stay in our old family houses which are now too big for us, but which were furnished by our wives and contain all our family memorabilia. Moving elsewhere would be a difficult decision for some of us that would involve a considerable break with the past.

On the other hand, our futures are unknown. Predictability of all phenomena is extremely low, and that applies particularly to populations, including the longevity of lives and marriages. At the time of our marriages, when male lives were much shorter, none of us would have ever imagined that our wives would predecease us, especially as most were younger and were expected to live longer. Moreover, readers of this book will realise that some men were widowed by the very abrupt death of their wife during the course of a single day, and suffered severe shock, while others watched their wife ail and disappear with dementia over very many years.

The challenge of adjustment

Over decades of marriage, most elderly widowers had become accustomed to separate marital roles and decision-making, which in many cases was much more striking than today when many more wives work. Taking over both roles often meant a total transformation of lifestyle, especially for those who had been little involved domestically. However, we all have different tales to tell. In general, through lack of practice elderly widowers cope less well domestically than elderly widows, but some adapt quite well especially those who take up cooking in a big way. Others rely on the very well prepared 'meals for one' that are now so readily available from major stores.

To change one's domestic situation requires a fairly dramatic stimulus, which of course may be provided by a new partner, companion or spouse. Because there are many more elderly women than men and more widows than widowers, the men have more possibilities should they so wish, but many prefer to have companions or partners rather than remarriage, with all the legal and family complications that implies.

We are conscious that the authors of this book are not an entirely representative sample, although finding such a sample would be very difficult as widowers have experienced such diverse lives. Generally they are positive persons determined to 'keep going' and anxious to make a contribution. Although men are often less good at mutual support than women, they enjoy the company of friends. Most of this sample have enough financially to stay put, keep going and don't have big expenses. Some can afford help in the home and garden if necessary, but are not seeking to transform or embellish their homes – that was done by their wives. They were family homes, and for that reason many don't want to move from them or downsize to live in a flat. In contrast, some widowers and many widows find themselves in less fortunate circumstances, especially for example when widows receive only half of their husbands' pensions and are forced to sell their homes and downsize, or find other means of increasing their incomes.

Curiously, 'widowerhood' does not appear in our dictionaries, and it has been called 'a taboo topic'. We hope that this short volume will offer some interest to many other widowers who are finding it hard to adjust to their changed circumstances.

Samuel Johnson:
My diseases are my asthma and a dropsy and, what is less curable, seventy-five.

Bob Hope:
I don't feel eighty. In fact I don't feel anything till noon. Then it's time for my nap.

Malcolm Muggeridge:
One of the pleasures of old age is giving things up.

Ogden Nash: *Senescence begins*
And middle age ends
The day your descendants
Outnumber your friends.

A. J. P .Taylor:
The greatest problem about old age is the fear that it may go on too long.

MORE ELDERLEY WIDOWERS
LIVING ALONE IN BRITAIN

An Ageing and Ageist Society

In the UK we are living in a rapidly ageing society, although social
acceptance of the older population is slow and less obvious than in
many of the societies of less advanced developing countries. Indeed,
Britain has a rather ageist or anti-aged society, valuing insufficiently
the roles of the elderly in all manner of ways such as in politics, the
economy and the media, where nowadays it is important to be
young or middle aged and good looking. Experience seems to matter
less and less; a telegenic style is valued more. This is evidenced
particularly among the political parties, where political leaders are
middle-aged and often have no other work experience while
politicians older than 60, despite being efficient (e.g. Vince Cable),
tend to be overlooked in the leadership stakes. Churchill, Gladstone
and Salisbury would not have succeeded in modern Britain.
Similarly, many older women who are still very capable but whose
youthful looks have diminished have found great difficulties in
maintaining their roles in public offices or on television
programmes. Too often the old are under-utilised by society, being
regarded as obsolescent and part of a 'dependency burden'.

The Rapidity of Ageing Increases with Age

As all individuals vary immensely, ageing is a very personal process.
There are no sharp thresholds of age, nationally or internationally.
Because the UK has a relatively high proportion of elderly people,
our definitions have differed a little from those of less advanced
countries. While for many years the UN has defined 'old' as 60 and

over, 'very old' as 75 and over and 'oldest old' as 80 and over, in the UK we have rather unusually used pensionable age to define the 'old' (curiously 65 for men and 60 for women, although women live longer), 75 and over for the 'very old', and 85 and over or sometimes 90 and over for the 'oldest old'. No doubt this has largely been because of our relatively high proportion of elderly people in comparison with many other countries, and their rapid increase in numbers during recent decades because they are living longer, despite their ailments.

Broadly speaking, the rapidity of growth of older age groups in the UK increases with the average age of the group. The percentage of the population aged 65 and over was only 5% in 1900, but it reached 16% in 2009 having grown by 1.7 million since 1983, and it is projected to be 23% in 2034 (Fig.1).

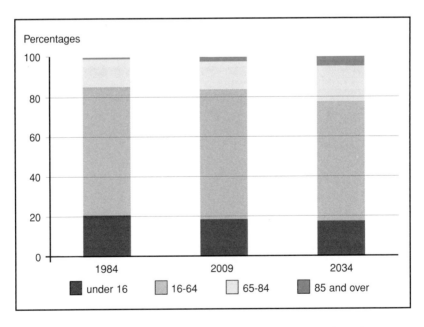

Fig. 1 – Increases in the aged population of the UK – 1984/2009/2034

Much more striking is the increasing number and percentage of the 'oldest old' aged 85 and over; in mid-2009 there were more than 1.4 million in the UK, 2.2% of the total population including 32% men, and it is projected that by 2034 they will number 3.5 million and account for as many as 5% of the total population.

Furthermore, as a result of better housing, health facilities and standards of living, the growth in the number of our centenarians has been even more impressive. In 1981 they numbered 2,600 in the UK, but by 2009 there were 11,600 (Fig.2) and almost incredibly they are projected to increase annually by as much as 8% to reach 87,900 in 2034 – surely too many for the Queen to send them all telegrams! In Scotland, however, where ageing is slightly less marked, centenarians represent a slightly lower percentage of the population.

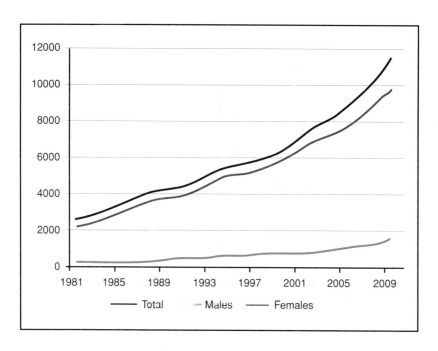

Fig. 2 – Growth in the number of male and female centurians in England and Wales, 1911-2009

Immigration Counters Ageing

It should be stressed that the surge of immigration of foreigners during this century has tended to act against the ageing of population, because most immigrants swell the younger adult age groups and many have children. Increases in the numbers of the elderly have largely resulted from changes in fertility and mortality over the last century and a half, but particularly since the middle of the twentieth century. The historic effects of high infant and child mortality have been greatly reduced, enabling people to live longer, and they have been replaced by new patterns of adult and aged mortality characterised by chronic and degenerative diseases, causing a transformation in the age structures of our populations. Consequently, during the 20th century the age structure of England and Wales changed from a pyramid-shape in 1901 to a bell-shape in 1951 and a bulb-shape in 2001 (Fig.3), as did the age structures of Scotland and Northern Ireland.

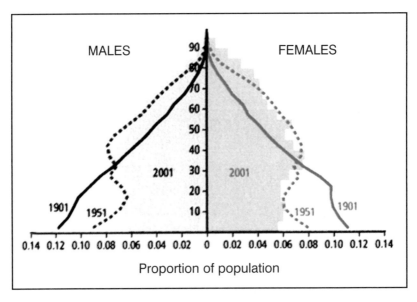

Fig.3 – The changing age-structure of England and Wales
1901, 1951 and 2001

On the other hand, while that largely reflected the preponderance of the white population, our Asian and mixed populations had much more youthful, broader-based age structures with fewer elderly people, while the age structure of the black population reflected more the number of recent adult immigrants.

Growing Number of Old Men

One aspect of this ageing process is that elderly men are living much longer than in the past, and are not quite so outnumbered by elderly women, at least among the less elderly aged groups. While elderly women have better life expectancy than elderly men, the gap between female and male life expectancy at birth in the UK diminished from 6.0 years in 1980-82 to 4.2 in 2007-09 (Fig.4), while at 65 the gap declined to only 2.6 years, the life expectancy of a woman being 23.8 years and that of a man 21.1.

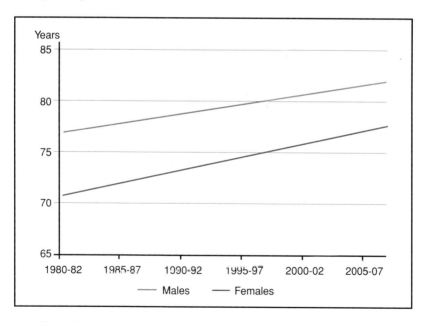

Fig.4 – Diminishing gap in female and male life expectancy in the UK, 1980-82 to 2005-07

The faster decline in elderly male mortality over the last few decades has mainly resulted from changes in their lifestyles, notably considerable reductions in noxious occupations (such as mining and heavy industry), smoking tobacco and in war casualties. Consequently, older women outnumber older men less markedly; the ratio of women to men aged 65 and over the UK has fallen from 156:100 in 1984 to 129:100 in 2009, and is projected to be only 118:100 in 2034. It has fallen slightly more steeply among the oldest old aged 85 and over, but the proportion of older women still increases quite sharply with age. Men are still much rarer among the highest age groups; women aged 90-99 currently outnumber men of that age by about three to one, while female centenarians outnumber males by as many as six to one. The overall numbers at that advanced age are of course much smaller and change quite a lot, but further falls in male mortality are expected to reduce the ratio.

Elderly People Living Alone

Single-person households now account for about three in ten of the increasing number of households in this country, but despite the growing numbers of elderly living alone they comprise a diminishing proportion of them. Back in 1971 elderly pensioners constituted two-thirds of the single-person households and non-pensionable adults one-third, but recent social and economic changes have caused the latter to increase so rapidly that adults and elderly now account for roughly half each of all single person households, and about 15% of all households. This striking social phenomenon of living alone in Britain has been caused by a number of major social and economic changes affecting the whole adult population:
  – an increasingly individualistic society with fewer family commitments;
  – less stigma in remaining unmarried or gay;
  – decline and delay in first marriage;
  – increase in marital separation and divorce;
  – longer journeys to work affecting the character of housing;
  – more readily available rented flats and maisonettes.

On the whole, however, the elderly living alone have a more diffuse geographic distribution than adults living alone, who tend to be especially attracted to large cities where more employment opportunities are available.

Differences between Elderly Men and Women Living Alone

Not surprisingly, strong differences occur between the frequencies of elderly men and women living alone. The preponderance of female one-person households increases markedly with age, especially because in general women outlive men, have older husbands or partners who predecease them, and have much lower rates of remarriage and higher rates of widowhood. It is also the case that the social and economic plight of widows is more difficult than that of widowers, as many have to survive on only half of their husband's pension, or worst of all on state pensions. They also suffer more from increasing isolation and segregation, particularly the relatively few living in some of the more remote rural areas of western 'Highland Britain', whose largely stable or declining populations generally tend to have more pensioners than the burgeoning populations of the more vibrant economic areas of eastern 'Lowland Britain' which have attracted younger labour from all over the country and from abroad.

In 2008, about 30% of women aged 65 and over in Great Britain lived alone compared with about 20% of men, but amongst the very elderly aged 75 and over the percentages are much higher: 61% for women, most of whom were widowed, divorced or separated, in comparison with 34% for men (Fig.5), although once again the proportions are very much lower within the Black British and Asian British populations which have been influenced more by recent immigration. Moreover, as women are more likely to be widowed than men, the proportion of very elderly women living in care or in medical establishments is generally at least double that of men, and it increases with age.

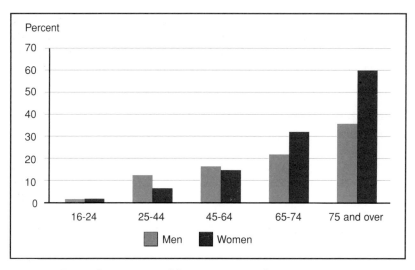

Fig.5 – Percentages of five age-groups of women and men
living alone in Great Britain, 2008

We should also remind ourselves that in 2001 one-fifth of all those
aged 85 and over in the UK lived in communal establishments.

The number of elderly men living alone is growing quickly, as they
are surviving better than in the past. This is partly due to the fact
that many have had relatively clean service occupations, have not
been affected by warfare, have given up smoking, experience
relatively balanced lives, and have outlived or separated from their
wives or partners. On the other hand, divorce and separation of the
elderly is increasing, and they are not always healthy; their total life
expectancy is rising more rapidly than their healthy life expectancy,
as both men and women are living longer lives with a limiting
illness or disability.

Under-occupancy of Housing

Many elderly men living alone also under-occupy their homes
where they formerly lived with wives and families, because the
problems of moving and creating new homes are perhaps seen as

more daunting by men than by women, who usually play greater roles in designing and furnishing family dwellings. Many men are too idle to move, or cannot face the associated problems. Sometimes this results in very low densities of occupation within detached and semi-detached housing estates, a fact which is seen in pockets in most of our cities. It has been particularly noticeable in some of our coastal resorts which have long acted as attractive retirement destinations. For example, southern coastal districts like East Devon, West Somerset, Bournemouth, Worthing and Eastbourne, which grew during the nineteenth and twentieth centuries as attractive summer holiday resorts but have suffered in recent decades through the growth of overseas travel to sunnier climes, offer varied types of accommodation as well as readily available leisure facilities to retirees. On the other hand, widowhood, individual isolation and advanced ageing generally reduce their attraction to elderly people living alone.

Social Participation

As British society tends to evolve with growing rapidity, so generation gaps are growing. Instead of three generations, there is a case for contending that there are more. Even the term 'seven ages of man' might now be increased to nine, corresponding to ten-year periods. Unfortunately, despite the increasing number of elderly men, they tend to command diminishing respect as society emphasises increasingly the popularity of youth, sport and fashion. Few elderly men retain major roles in any organisation; most tend to play only minor roles which reduce markedly with age. Those living alone tend to play even smaller roles and be less integrated, partly because they have to look after themselves. Many decades ago, Anthony Powell went so far as to say that 'growing old is like being increasingly penalised for a crime you haven't committed'.

The usual retirement age of 65 affects most working and non-working lives, enforcing a profound change of life particularly for elderly men whether they want it or not. Although a few firms like Sainsbury's and B&Q are more benevolent to the elderly, even voluntary activities are often affected, as many public bodies shy away from committee members aged over 70. Fortunately, numerous charities are not so socially discriminating, and employ the manifold abilities of the elderly because salaries are normally not involved. Many elderly gain great pleasure and interest in fulfilling a need, and without them many charities would suffer.

Despite such activities, there is a strong case for suggesting that society takes insufficient note of the abilities of its elderly male population, many of whom could contribute very much more.

All figures were created by the Office of National Statistics

"COME BACK, DARLING — ALL IS FORGIVEN!"

Cartoon by David Haldane after Steven Berry;
we are grateful to both.

Alan Taylor

My wife's death

My wife, who shall be identified as Z, died in 1983 after an illness of eleven months. I was very distressed, but my grief for her was diverted when eight days later my mother died. Because of these two deaths, I was absent from employment for almost two weeks. I always remember a lady telling me to concentrate my thoughts on my work, and when I returned to my job this is what I did; it occupied my mind and diverted my thoughts from sad and unhappy events.

Living alone and friends

Z had cared for me in a superb manner: well fed and a comfortable home. One thing that concerned me was how I would feel about coming home after a day's work to an empty house with no meal ready and having to prepare food. It was not a happy experience and it took me several weeks to adjust to this change in lifestyle. I had lunched at home each day when Z was alive and now I had to lunch at a restaurant or hotel, but with two sons living at home I prepared meals for them at weekends.

With the assistance of a good friend, I acquired the services of a lady cleaner who came to my home twice a week and kept the house tidy and under control; she was a great help and relieved me of a worry. Shopping did not present a major problem as I had accompanied Z on many shopping expeditions in the past.

Friends that I knew were very kind and helpful; they brought me home-made pies and cakes and invited me to their homes for a meal. I always accepted these invitations with alacrity as it was such a pleasure to be in the company of other people in their comfortable homes – it made me feel better and lifted the gloom in my heart. In my employment I was 'the boss' and worked very hard to fill my mind with problems other than grief.

Memories

I had clear and strong memories of my last year with Z, and during quiet moments I would sadly think of what she and I were doing on a particular day twelve months previously. I could not help or avoid recalling these events and it made me miserable. These unhappy reminiscences occurred frequently especially on birthdays and anniversaries and continued to trouble me until eighteen months after Z's death. Then one day visiting the Roman Wall with my younger son I realised that these recollections and thoughts were not helping me, and I decided to make a determined effort to stop looking back to what I had done with Z, and instead to live in the present and look to the future. I started to attend social functions with mixed company, and although it saddened me that I did not have a partner I still enjoyed myself. Only when it was time to return home did the lack of a partner trouble me.

However, the absence of my wife in my home was a great loss: no one with whom to talk, to share worries or to go on holidays. I was fortunate with holidays as a couple of friends, husband and wife, asked me to go on holidays with them for several years. Friends have been kind to me, and I am thankful for their concern and for giving me the pleasure of their company and hospitality.

Retirement

I retired from employment five years after Z's death and started to build a new life. I ceased to look back to years with my wife, something I did with difficulty but after the first year of being on my own it became easier as I had accumulated another year of events, memories and recollections which diminished the effects of those first twelve unhappy months when I missed Z's company and love immensely and when I was out of the big picture of life.

Widowhood is not a happy experience, but the passage of years gradually diminishes the sorrow and grief. I often felt that I was fortunate in having to rise every day and go to work, and to concentrate my thoughts on my duties and tasks. Without that escape my sorrow would have become more deeply concentrated in my mind.

21

Arnold Wolfendale

Marriage, dementia and death

My wife Audrey died in March 2007; we had been happily married since February 1951. We met when I was 17 and she was 18, and she was the only girlfriend I ever had; it was love at first sight, and thus we 'grew up' together. Twin sons Colin and David arrived in December 1952, and we became very proud of their achievements, and eventually those of their spouses and children. We were always a happy, united family; we still are.

Audrey developed Alzheimer's some 13 years before she died, and spent the last four and a half years in care homes. Prior to that I had looked after her at home, but my boys were anxious that she should go into care.

Audrey's closest friend, 'Little Audrey', a widow neglected by her family, helped me to look after Audrey when she was at home and frequently visited her in the care home(s). We held Audrey's hands when she passed away, and Little Audrey's presence made life worth living and our mutual love eased the pain. However, early in 2010 she too deteriorated into dementia, and she is now in care herself; a case of *déjà-vu* if there ever was one. Near-daily visits have become the norm again.

Academic and artistic activities

A constant activity, which has not diminished over the past 60+ years, has been my personal research within the university. Having been head of the Physics Department for 10 years on and off, and worked hard to introduce Astronomy after a gap of 70 years, I was and still am *persona grata* which means that I still have a room in the Department plus the usual secretarial, reprographic and computing facilities. I like to think that the quality of my research in astrophysics and climate change is as good as ever. Certainly honours (medals, honorary degrees, named lectures and such like) continue to flow, and I hope to continue researching to the end.

Despite my obsession with research, I have taken time off to take an interest in art, particularly in 'art and science'. This has led to nearly filling my house with art by (often) local artists, and to lecturing on the topic. I am a patron of an art college in London, as well as of a number of other bodies (Friends of the Durham Oriental Museum, Durham Dramatic Society). I still lecture about once a month to an amateur body somewhere and attend conferences. My presidency of the Antiquarian Horological Society also gives me pleasure, and I hope them too.

Friends, relatives and religion

Being of a lazy disposition regarding domestic chores, I have a weekly cleaner and gardener. Indeed, one of the gardeners is now a personal friend. Friends in the university and town abound, and their friendship helps to fill the undoubted void. Since Alzheimer's struck, I have 'turned up the wick' with entertaining at home (and its reciprocation). I work on the principle of 'having a big house, I'd better use it'.

When my prayers for Audrey's recovery from Alzheimer's were not answered and the clergy couldn't care less, I left the Cathedral and became an atheist. Indeed, I may join the humanists. In October 2010, I debated 'The existence of God: the case for and against' (I was against!) with my old student Rev. Dr. David Wilkinson in the presence of a Cathedral audience of about 600, and the roof did not fall in – showing that I was right! I am currently awaiting replies to my challenges from the Chief Rabbi and the Archbishop of Canterbury. My son David, a church warden, says 'Why do you do this father?' I sometimes wonder myself.

Service to others

From the age of nine to sixteen I was a Boy Scout, and I loved every minute of my scouting. In retrospect, membership probably kept me on the straight and narrow. The ethos of 'service to others' took root at an early age, and I have endeavoured to keep it up. Having fancy titles and being a confidant of many of 'the good and the great' has helped considerably in the past couple of decades to ensure that worthy colleagues have been honoured in various ways (FRS, OBEs, knighthoods, honorary degrees and such like). I have obtained as much pleasure from these rather lengthy activities as from my purely personal honours. Had I been a Lloyd George I would have been, by now, a very wealthy man!

Family and future

This brings me to my family. I see them every few months only, but speak quite frequently on the phone. They are my supporters, but I encourage them to live their own lives. My five grown-up grandchildren are doing well; two are married (Caroline and Alison) and Richard will marry in June 2011; Hilary the youngest is a 4th year medical student at my old University of Manchester; and Clare is in the NHS.

I have told the boys to 'put the boot in' if I show signs of mental decay; I have seen too much of care homes to want to go there. David and his wife want me to move in with them if and when, but I don't want to leave Durham. Sherburn House, where I lecture every month, is a more likely residence, although a short sharp heart attack is preferred.

What then of the quality of life of an elderly widower living alone? It could be a lot worse, is my reply. The Nobel Prize in 2012 (the centenary of Viktor Hess's discovery of cosmic rays) would be appreciated and would represent a *grande finale!*

Memories

Inevitably at 83 and living alone, memories play a part in one's life. My attempts to focus on happy times have so far been successful. Walking past the small wooded cemetery where I scattered Audrey's ashes four times a day keeps her memory alive. Time after time I think about very early days when we were both students and our romance was blossoming. Again, thoughts about my sons tend to focus on their childhood. Similarly with Little Audrey; even though she is still here, it is the early days that register most frequently. The psychologists no doubt will have an explanation.

My life seems to have been devoted to giving advice! As the 14th Astronomer Royal (1991-5), part of my 'job description' was 'to advise the Government'. This I did with gusto, and without it being solicited, about the parlous state of funding for science in the UK. The advice was not appreciated at all by HMG, but the media loved it! No doubt the following few words will not be appreciated either:

● Look on the bright side, there is always someone in more difficulty than you are.

● In intellectual pursuits show these youngsters that you are their equal, or better. In my view, our increased experience outweighs modest memory loss.

● Keep your eyes open for a rich, lovely widow – your late wife would be proud of you (I think).

Don Gelson

Durham born and bred

I have lived and worked in County Durham all my life. Born in Willington in 1932, I left school at 14, just after the war when few jobs were available. Initially I hated so much working in factories, but at 17 I moved to work on a large Brancepeth private estate where I stayed until I was married.

My wife Betty and I first met at the Astoria dance hall in Silver Street Durham, 60 years before she died. She was actually born in Silver Street, was two years younger than me, and we courted for five years. One regular event was when Betty used to make sure that I got on the 10.50pm last bus to Willington. When it was full with a number of soldiers travelling to Brancepeth camp, I would borrow Betty's father's bike if he was not using it for a nightshift at the pit; otherwise I would have to walk the eight miles home.

Betty and I were married in 1955 and lived very happily together for 55 years. We did everything and went everywhere together, along with our daughter Angela in the early days. After marriage, I joined Durham County Council's schools ground staff, and then left for 15 years as a gardener in the private sector before returning to the Council staff for the rest of my working career.

We enjoyed our holidays, including three coach tours in America and Canada, and others in Europe and the UK. When we were both retired, we tried to plan a holiday break as often as possible. We would recommend in particular the snow coaches. On one occasion hazardous snow conditions in the Italian Dolomites led to snow chains being attached to the coach tyres to negotiate a steep hill, which made it all the more exciting. Our last snow coach was in Switzerland 2009.

Our most memorable holiday was in Australia, climbing the Sydney Harbour Bridge, a challenge for both of us as it was for my 70th birthday. It is good to look back at the photographs – very happy memories.

Betty's sudden death

Betty's death was so abrupt, unexpected and shocking, as she died very suddenly on 2nd May, 2010. We had just come back from a five-day holiday, and were out celebrating Angela's 50th birthday. We were in a pub waiting to be called for dinner, when Betty's arm suddenly twisted and her face contorted with a severe aneurism. I remember saying to Angela "Oh dear, your mam's having a stroke", and of course there was a terrible commotion as people were having their meals and an ambulance was called to take her to hospital. There she had a scan, which was e-mailed through to Newcastle for a second opinion, but the aneurism was so massive that the consultant sadly told me that she had only hours to live – in fact, she lasted only five. An awful moment was removing her jewellery, although of course it was given to Angela.

In Durham news travels fast, and a large number of friends and family attended her funeral service in St Giles Church, Gilesgate followed by cremation at Durham Crematorium, particularly members of the Caravan Club of which we had been members for 32 years and I had been an officer and committee member for some of that time. Everyone was so kind, but Angela and I felt so bereft that all the arrangements had to be made by my son-in-law, Jim. Shortly afterwards, the crematorium personnel asked if we wanted a plaque on the wall of remembrance, but we decided that we don't need anything like that to remember her, as we have lots of fond memories, photographs and videos of our time together.

Adjustment

Her death is still dominant part of my life, as we were so very close, doing everything together. It was devastating to donate her clothes to charity; many bags were filled and left to a number of collectors, I am very lucky that my daughter Angela and son-in-law Jim live only a few hundred yards away, and that I have good neighbours and friends. Although I have sold my caravan, I still keep in touch with caravanning friends. Durham is also a good place for social mixing.

During our marriage, Betty had done all the paper work for us, and I knew little about our affairs, so I had a lot to learn, even simple things like writing a cheque and the differences between credit and debit cards and between savings and current accounts. I had to go to the bank to find out what was coming in and going out, like pensions, direct debits, council tax, income tax and general expenses. It was quite an ordeal. And there were also visits to the solicitor about wills. Even shopping for myself became a problem, which is very strange, as I tended to buy for two.

Ready meals do fill a void, and are easy and convenient. I am also finding the benefits of a slow cooker; the freezer is becoming full of soup, which is no bad thing in the winter months. I now have a recipe book so I can try to expand my slow cooker knowledge. In addition, I found that domestic chores are very time-consuming: washing (I quickly learnt about separating whites from colours), ironing, cleaning, etc... I now know what they mean when they say that 'a woman's work is never done'.

I am recording in photographs the 'changing face of Durham market place, 2009-11' from the start of the alterations to the market place, the tedious task of the removal and replacement of the statue of Lord Londonderry on his horse (always referred to as 'the horse') and the upgrading of the pedestrian walkway to the final completion in 2011. Betty was there at the start of the alterations, showing a keen but not always approving interest; regretfully she is not here to witness the completion.

I still go down 'memory lane' where we met at the Astoria dance hall. It is now an outdoor clothing store, and some of the staff were surprised when I mentioned that I met my wife there sixty years ago, as not all of them knew that there used to be a dance hall upstairs.

One good thing I did in October 2010 was to go on a week's coach tour to Austria, where Betty and I had holidayed many times in the past. Although I was upset when we crossed the border into Austria, I am glad that I went, as I made new friends – one of the great benefits of a coach tour is that at the start you are strangers, but some end up as friends before arriving home.

It brought home to me our philosophy regarding holidays: if you can afford it and have the time, do it. Now as a single traveller I have to consider the single supplements that travel companies feel the need to charge us, some of which I find exorbitant.

It is now approaching Christmas, the first year that I have had to write the Christmas cards, which was a job done always by Betty. Luckily she had a list of all those to whom we send cards, which made the task easier, as I don't want to leave anyone out. It is surprising that of all the friends and relations we have, we must not have notified all of her death as some cards are addressed to us both, which can be quite upsetting to both parties, especially when I send my card and notify them of her death. A Happy or Merry Christmas does not have the same meaning.

We have been told and understand that the first year is always the hardest, as you go through the first time for everything. They say that life gets easier, and here's hoping it will. As time goes on I hope that I will be able to cope without interfering with my daughter's life, although I know that she would do her best for me.

Gerald Blake

First thoughts

The more I have observed and chatted to friends about it, the more I have come to realise that huge differences exist between individuals in their preparedness for life alone. All of us have some assets to help us through the years of being alone, but few embark on the journey fully equipped. This is no surprise: we do not spend our married lives preparing to be widowers, and there is a strong inclination in all of us to believe that we will be able to keep things going much as they always were, so practical adjustments which might have been put in place are postponed.

What might be the profile of a widower (say in his seventies), who is ideally equipped to make the most of life on his own? In addition to the obvious requirements of an adequate pension and reasonably good health, I suggest the following ten factors: (1) he lives in manageable accommodation, not too large, and equipped for ease of cleaning, comfort, economy and convenience; (2) he is sufficiently mobile to get out and about without undue assistance; (3) he has a number of friends with whom he maintains regular contact, and as a bonus he has friendly and caring neighbours; (4) he belongs to a club, church, society or the like which offer opportunities for socialising, and the continuation of an element of service in the community; (5) he has a supportive family, preferably within easy reach; (6) he has adequate domestic skills and is comfortable preparing meals; (7) he has some well developed leisure interests, the more absorbing the better, whether painting, collecting, reading, research, golf, gardening or whatever; (8) he is able to use a computer at least for e-mailing and surfing the internet; (9) he takes adequate exercise and eats wisely; and (10) throughout the year he makes sure there is some event in his diary to look forward to, such as a holiday, a family visit, a weekend away or a day at the seaside.

There could of course be all kinds of additional criteria to those listed above. For example, some might suggest the benefits of keeping pets, but the point here is that nobody is ideally equipped for life alone. As a totally unscientific exercise, try taking the ten suggested indicators and mark yourself out of five for each. A score of 50 is inconceivable, 40 would be very good, but most of us will probably score far less. On some indicators, our scores might be high, on others very low. In other words, everybody has some assets, but few have them all. It showed me personally that I should be grateful for the assets I have, and perhaps consider what to do about those where I fall short.

To date, my experience of living alone has been very positive. I will be 75 by the time anybody reads this. I lost my wife Brenda to cancer in 2007, after 40 years of married life. In general I have a fulfilling and very happy life. There are frustrations and disappointments of course, and as the years go by there are activities I can no longer manage, or dare not attempt. At the same time I have taken up new challenges, such as a return to regular swimming once a week or more, and I have become involved in new activities in the community such as joining the Friends of the Bowes Museum. If asked what I regard as the single most important ingredient in my contentment, it would have to be my Christian faith. I do not expect everybody to understand this, but it remains a fact that my daily walk with God means that I do not feel alone, and the shape of my future and my destiny after death are the business of One who loves me, and ultimately there is nothing to fear. What I write below is inevitably coloured by these personal beliefs.

Family

I have three adult children: a married son and two daughters (one single, and one married). My son lives in Tynemouth, about 90 minutes away by road. I stay with him and my daughter-in-law two or three times a year, and they similarly come to Romaldkirk. My married daughter and her husband and my one granddaughter live in Sevenoaks, about six or seven hours away by road. My other daughter has worked most of her professional life in the south of England and Scotland. In other words none of my family lives on the doorstep, but they are all accessible and they make an effort to meet and communicate at least two or three times a year, often on holidays. My Sevenoaks family like renting holiday cottages, and kindly often invite me to join them, which I much enjoy. Besides my own children, I am in regular touch with my two brothers and sister, all of whom live in the south and west of England. They are a great source of advice, support and of funny stories that are very important to me, and I cannot understand how some people completely lose touch with their siblings.

House and garden

My home is a three bedroom stone cottage in Teesdale. It is comfortable enough, and externally it appears very attractive to visitors to the village. As with all old buildings there is no end to ways of spending money on maintenance and improvements. I wish we had done more alterations when we first acquired the property as a retreat in 1991. The heating comes from an old Rayburn in the kitchen which is not very efficient, but I love its year-round warmth, and I am reluctant to change it. The decision to replace an open fire in the lounge with a log-burning stove was inspired. It brings cheer and warmth, is safe, and if managed well, quite economical. I wish we had it plumbed into the hot water system, as the house insulation would be better and overall heating costs not so high and rising.

At present I am able to enjoy my Teesdale residence to the full. I love the house and I love Teesdale, but I am not blind to bears lurking behind trees to ambush me in future. There is no garage, so I am short of storage space, and I often have to scrape frost and snow from my car on winter mornings. The stairs are steep and narrow, and there is no walk-in shower or internal downstairs toilet. A very small garden to the front of the house and a small enclosed one to the rear mean that vegetables can only be grown on a small scale in pots. Keeping a dog no longer seems to be a sensible option. We enjoyed the company of black Labradors for 23 years but they were walked by my wife or by me three times a day. Sadly I feel unable to make that commitment again, although still think about it. I try to keep both gardens colourful and tidy, especially the front garden which is part of a much photographed and painted village scene, alongside the church and overlooking the green. Although my gardens are small, there are more than enough gardening tasks in them to keep me amused and give me backache whenever I wish.

I like to think that I did my fair share of household chores while my wife was alive, but after she had gone I appreciated what she had done more than ever. However I was determined not to allow standards to slip, so after some months working alone I began to pay a cleaner for a couple of hours a week. This wonderful lady whizzed round most of the house leaving it smelling of polish and looking great. She helped clear out cupboards, made curtains and duvet covers, and re-potted my ailing peace lilies and geraniums. She was a terrific source of local news and gossip and I looked forward to her visits until ill-health forced her to retire in September 2010. She undoubtedly helped me through a critical three years of adjustment and reorganisation, and I was very fortunate to have her help and advice for that time.

I used to do a fair amount of DIY jobs and decorating in the house, and continue to do what I can. With loads of tools, the results of my DIY endeavours are probably no worse than before, but I tend to suffer from painful knees and a stiff back after sustained DIY activity, which rather dampens my former enthusiasm. I am also more cautious when scaling ladders and using sharp tools while alone in the house. My wife was a trained nurse and first-aid instructor, and it was reassuring to know that she was on hand in the event of mishap. In fact I cannot recall being involved in any serious DIY injury, unlike some of my friends whose DIY antics have ended in appalling accidents. I am pleased to say that Teesdale is blessed with some excellent tradesmen who are skilled and reliable, and I have made good use of their services, especially stonemasons.

Domestic skills

I was sufficiently well domesticated to be able to cope quite well after my wife died. I could iron a shirt (national service taught me that), sew on buttons, and clean the house. As for cooking, I could prepare some basic meals including roasts, mixed grills, fish pies, and egg and cheese dishes, and love to assemble and eat salads. There was therefore never any danger of starving. Well-meaning family members gave me a bread making machine, a smoothie maker, and a small library of cookbooks, but these have been underutilised. In the three and a half years of living alone I have scarcely enhanced my cooking skills, and my diet has included much the same range of familiar dishes and ready-made meals from the supermarkets.

By good fortune I was prevented from slipping further into bad habits by a personal friend whose professional advice I sought early in 2010. Before offering any advice she required me to keep a detailed 'food diary' for 14 days, which I did as accurately as I could. She was horrified by the resulting evidence of snacking on sugary things, irregular times of eating, too few green vegetables, too little fluid, and an unfavourable acid/alkaline balance. With her skilful guidance and encouragement, I have tried to rectify my wicked ways, and have felt the benefit of her advice. I have lost weight, and eat more sensibly than a year ago. Weight loss was assisted by taking regular exercise, usually a 40-60 minute brisk walk each day, and swimming at least once a week. Although unlikely to win any cookery competitions, and my fridge and larder shelves are unlikely to excite serious foodies, I now eat reasonably healthily (with occasional lapses), and highly recommend keeping a food diary for a couple of weeks, even if it is not seen by an expert. You may be surprised at what (and when) you are eating.

While touching on health matters, I should say that I sleep very well at night apart from the usual trip (or trips) to the bathroom. I have made a big effort to ensure good sleep by investing in very good quality duvets and pillows, and buying a wonderfully comfortable Tempur mattress. I have secondary glazing throughout the house which reduces external noise in the bedrooms, although my village is normally quiet. I like to sleep in a very dark room so I have roller blinds and curtains to give the desired effect. Writing a page of the day's happenings in a diary last thing at night in bed probably also helps me sleep, and when it is done, the day is done, and its happenings can be closed and concluded. Looking back at these records, I am sometimes astonished to see how much I managed to fit into a single day, and sometimes I am dismayed that nothing seemed to have been achieved.

Getting about

I am fortunate that I can still drive a car (and can still just about afford to run it) which is virtually essential for life in rural Teesdale, although there are elderly people in the village who have no vehicles and have found other ways of shopping and accessing services. One day no doubt I will have to face up to doing the same; shopping with Tesco online twice has shown it can be done! The nearest shops and the doctor's surgery are four miles away in Middleton in Teesdale, but for most of my shopping Barnard Castle (some six miles away) is preferable. My bank (I still prefer traditional banking) and dentist are 17 miles away in Bishop Auckland. I still travel to Durham (58 miles round trip) fairly often to see friends, attend events and meetings, and for occasional rowing coaching. It is worth mentioning that I believe I extended my rowing coaching life by investing in a far superior and more expensive bicycle than the model I had been using, which saw me struggling to keep up with the faster crews (and they are all seemingly getting quicker!)

Driving at night is not very enjoyable, largely because oncoming lights seem so bright. At one time I used to travel long distances overnight from choice, but no more. I continue to make long road journeys to destinations in the south several times each year, clocking up approximately 18,000 miles annually, much to the surprise of my insurance company. Without my wife to share these journeys and help with driving, I find long journeys increasingly stressful. My solution is to break the journeys overnight with friends or at a Travelodge or Premier Inn, which I quite enjoy. I still miss my wife to help navigate. She was a superb map reader, who liked to sit down and 'read' OS maps for pleasure. I have drawers full of her map collection. As soon as we joined a tailback on the motorways she would propose diverting down country roads, lanes and farm tracks to avoid the traffic. The results were rarely a big success, but as she argued "at least we are moving and not breathing those deadly fumes". I had to agree.

Although I used to be a frequent traveller abroad (I once calculated that I have been to around 60 countries), my appetite for foreign travel has almost entirely been lost. I am rather surprised about this myself. It might return, but as things stand I am not planning to travel abroad much in the foreseeable future. Many of my trips abroad were for research, conferences or lecturing, so I was usually travelling alone. I would happily holiday alone abroad if I felt so inclined, but do not. I simply wish to avoid the stress (as I perceive it) of modern travel, and make more of the United Kingdom for holidays. In 2009 I spent a memorable week in Naples while my son was working there. I rather hope my appetite for travel abroad will revive because there are several people I have promised to visit, and places I would dearly like to see. High on my list is the part of India where my mother was born and lived with her missionary parents until she was 10 years old. I have never been on a cruise, but might try it some day on the recommendation of friends who are completely hooked on the experience.

For holidays, I generally go to the two timeshare properties which we bought some years ago on Tresco (Isles of Scilly) and Underscar (near Keswick). Happily all my family love to come to these beautiful places when possible. Neither place can accommodate all of us at the same time, but we always manage to make them a focus for some of the family each year, and much enjoy each other's company. Tresco is one of the most tranquil and beautiful places I know anywhere on earth, and it works its magic on me every year. My wife Brenda also adored Tresco and we had our last holiday together there in 2006. Partly for this reason there come moments on every visit when I feel her loss more acutely than almost anywhere else. Brenda would be pleased that we continue to go on our Tresco holidays.

I also make an annual visit to Henley Royal Regatta, generally staying for three or four days out of five days of racing. It is one of the highlights of my year. I go to watch rowing (which is not necessarily the top priority for some visitors!), but also revel in the chance to meet old friends, enjoy good food, and absorb the atmosphere. If the sun shines, it is just perfect. I believe we all need something to look forward to, and for me the prospect of another Henley at the end of June and early July is marvellous. My allocation of tickets generally arrives before winter is out, lifting my spirits no end.

Social life

I try to prune my Christmas card list each year but it remains quite long. It includes good friends going back to school, national service and university days, as well as many I got to know during my time in Durham through the university and St Nicholas church in the Market Place. I value all these longstanding friendships. Closer examination of my Christmas card list reveals that in 2010 I had met only about 45 of those to whom I sent cards, while I had eaten a meal during the year with only 24 of them. All this suggests that I need to invest more time and effort in the old friends I value, or recognise that they are part of the past and let them go. I also looked at my card list and asked myself how many of them I would turn to in a serious crisis, or for personal advice. I was gratified to identify 15-20 in this category. I believe these are the friends I need to nurture and keep in touch with above all. A friend of mine who recognised that he was losing touch with valued friends decided to make a grand tour of Britain to re-establish contact with them. It was a great success, except that word went round that he was dying (which he was not) and was coming round to say goodbye!

I joined the Barnard Castle Rotary Club in 2004 and was introduced at once to a circle of new friends. The club numbers 30 men and women, all of whom know the Barnard Castle area well, and through them I have met other local people. My wife had joined the Club the year before me and would have been our first woman president, but she died four months before inauguration. When my turn came to be President I did it in honour of her. In the months when she was seriously ill I received great support and friendship from fellow Rotarians. Of course, Rotary is far more than a social organisation, and I have been involved in fund-raising events of all kinds, helping to find speakers, and assisting with service projects, among which conducting mock interviews in local schools is most enjoyable. Through its weekly meetings over dinner and practical service, Rotary has encouraged me to get out and about regularly, to meet other people, and open up windows on the world. I have attended two Rotary residential conferences and greatly enjoyed the opportunity to meet Rotarians from all over the North East.

I attend church as regularly as possible. The village congregations are small but they include several people from the village who have become personal friends. When my wife and I took up permanent residence in the village when I retired in 2001, it was the people we met in church who made us feel at home. We would probably have achieved the same result if we had made regular visits to either of the two pubs in the village, both of which are within 100 metres or so of our front door.

Apart from family when they come to stay, I have not attempted very much entertaining since my wife died in 2007 despite always intending to do so, not least because a number of friends have been very kind in extending hospitality to me. The reason I have done so little is partly laziness, and partly trepidation. As mentioned above, good friendships have to be nurtured and kept alive, and I feel a failure in this endeavour. I have sometimes invited friends to join me for a meal in a favourite restaurant, and must do that more often because it is fun. I am fortunate to have a large circle of friends which includes couples and single men and women. One woman in particular has become a close friend, and her company at various events is always a special pleasure when it can be arranged.

I use the internet to keep in touch with friends and colleagues, but have maintained the art of writing letters and cards. I do not (yet?) have Skype, do not twitter, am not on Facebook, do not blog, and do not (yet?) have Sky TV. Admirable as they may be, I do not expect to adopt any of these means of communication in the immediate future.

Leisure interests

I rather wish I had developed a passion for some creative hobby or leisure interest during my working life, which would have taken off in retirement and carried on past bereavement. It is not that I have too little to do; on the contrary I keep very busy and am never bored. I have never joined U3A or Probus because of lack of time. I simply feel the need to fall back on a single all-absorbing activity which might satisfy certain creative urges. My elderly friends make stained glass windows, paint pictures, make silverware, blow glass, collect hats, grow bonsai trees, collect medals, make chutney and write poetry. I had several recreational interests when I retired, but they were mostly only partially developed or had lain dormant for years. After retirement therefore I made excursions into family history (some success), the history of rowing, and the geography of the

Bible. I dabbled in oil and watercolour painting. I was given books on digital photography, chutney making, Mediterranean cooking, antique maps, and tying knots, because I had foolishly indicated an interest in these pursuits at some time or other. Any one of these, if followed with commitment, might have proved wonderfully rewarding, but unfortunately I never got down to it. I do not believe it is too late to start again, and family history is at the top of my list.

In the past three years I have been largely responsible for the co-ordination and presentation of two exhibitions which took a lot of time and proved to be very exciting. The first was at the River and Rowing Museum in Henley-on-Thames in 2008 to commemorate 175 years of Durham University rowing, and the second was at the Witham Hall in Barnard Castle in connection with the 70th anniversary of the Rotary Club of Barnard Castle. We invited the public to bring items from their homes which might be of interest, and the resulting exhibition was truly amazing. These projects were hair-raising experiences, but they brought me in contact with all kinds of people I had not met before and faced me with unusual challenges. I am hoping to help with another exhibition commemorating local sporting heroes in time for Olympic year, but the necessary support is still being sought.

I read books and newspapers, attempting the easy crosswords most days, and have a substantial book collection of my own. One of my best purchases in recent months was a *'Serious Reader'* reading light. It has transformed my reading habits, enabling me to read far longer than before without eyestrain. Highly recommended! I feel sure that being as well equipped as possible is one of the keys to remaining active for as long as possible.

Last thoughts

It was most useful to have been asked to share my thoughts about living alone. I had never really weighed up the assets and liabilities which together have shaped my current way of life. Having done so, I feel very fortunate. A caring family and continuing friendships and social contacts have (to date) enabled me to make the most of life alone. My intention is to ensure by whatever practical means the continuation of a happy and fulfilling life. This will involve more thought and planning, possibly alterations in the house, and investing time in getting about and maintaining contacts. All this will take more and more effort as the years go by, but I intend to follow the example of so many fellow travellers, and never give up.

James Freeley

Marriage

My wife Maeve and I met in Dublin at a local tennis club dance in 1951. Following our engagement, we were married in September 1954, spent our honeymoon in the Lake District and then moved into our first home, a semi-detached bungalow in South County Dublin.

We were blessed with three sons, one of whom, Ronan, lives in Durham. My second, Declan, now lives in Lagos Nigeria where I have three grandsons, and my youngest son Conall lives in London.

Career

Following a sales marketing career in Dublin with the local office of National Cash Register Co., in 1970 I joined the UK subsidiary of a Dutch company manufacturing PVC pipes. This involved moving to Preston Lancashire without my family, so I commuted between Preston and Dublin on a weekly basis. That company took over another PVC company who had a factory in Durham City, where my family joined me in 1973.

One of my ambitions was to start my own business, and fortunately I had that opportunity in 1975. My wife and I were joint directors and it proved to be successful and profitable. On reaching the age of sixty, I received an approach from a supplier to purchase the business as a going concern, and we decided to accept and sell it in 1988.

Dementia

Our life as a retired couple was very happy, and we celebrated our golden wedding anniversary in September 2004, but late in 2003 my wife was diagnosed with dementia for which she was prescribed Aricept to reduce its effects.

From then I undertook the role of carer. Initially this was not arduous, but as time passed her memory was deteriorating. In addition, she could not manage to go out on her own, as she was not aware of any danger. Further effects of her illness became obvious. We decided to avail ourselves of a paid carer, which involved a daily one-hour visit for five mornings, excluding weekends, to assist Maeve with dressing and showering. All the other household tasks were dealt with by me. However, my wife did not enjoy this intrusion into her private life, and subsequently we dispensed with their poor service. I then took on the full carer role, which I was pleased to do. At that time she was more relaxed, and we spent many happy hours together.

As the months passed she was falling during the day, and more frequently at night. It was very difficult to move her, but I had to make her as comfortable as possible lying on the floor until I could summon assistance of the ambulance service or that of my son. As time passed it was apparent that she needed 24-hour care, and in September 2007 she became quite immobile and doubly incontinent.

Following a short stay in hospital, we agreed to apply for a respite period in Hallgarth Care Home in Durham City. This enabled me to visit her every day and have some private time when I arranged to take her out to lunch, afternoon tea and short car journeys. While she was happy and relaxed, her general condition continued to deteriorate. She became increasingly immobile and had to use a walking frame or wheelchair. We were informed that she was suffering mini-strokes, which were observed by the staff on a regular basis.

The Reader Organisation

In February 2008, I read an article in *The Guardian* by Blake Morrison about *The Reader Organisation* in Liverpool founded by Dr Jane Davis, in which she had developed reading groups in the North-West of England in care homes, drug rehabilitation centres and in hospitals dealing with mental illness. Her experience and anecdotal evidence showed how people with a wide range of problems, including dementia, could benefit by reading and listening to qualified people reading literature and poetry; she had called this *'bibliotherapy'*. I phoned Dr Davis to enquire about a training course, and discussed the matter with the management of Hallgarth Care Home and their dementia consultant, who agreed to a three-month trial subject to anecdotal evidence being made available and supervision by a senior nurse. Then I attended a five-day course on the Wirral and received a certificate accredited by the University of Liverpool. We held our first meeting of the Hallgarth Poetry Group in April 2008 and Maeve became a regular contributor.

Following her death on 27th November 2008, I decided to continue my role as a facilitator in Hallgarth Care Home. The group is now a permanent part of the recreational programme, and has at least ten residents at each session as well as university student visitors. We are in discussion with the parent company Southern Cross Healthcare Ltd, who operate over 700 similar care homes throughout the UK, to extend the programme to others in the company. The Poetry Group will be three years old in April 2011, and its results and benefits are remarkable as there is a great feeling of enthusiasm, improved memory, wellbeing and self-confidence.

Living alone as a widower

Despite an awareness of a sad conclusion to an extended illness of my life partner, there was an air of unreality with little time to plan the details. I was shocked for some time to adjust to a major change in my lifestyle. Fortunately my eldest son was living in Durham, which brought us closer together. I was involved in the Hallgarth reading group on a fortnightly basis, but initially I found it very difficult calling into the Hallgarth within weeks of her passing, and looking at the chair she used on the first floor. However, I received great consolation from my close friends, Rotarian colleagues and other friends in my local church.

I was fortunate to obtain the services of an excellent home help to guide me on the basic domestic chores, and decided to continue with my newly established routines of rising at a fixed time. In general, I kept myself busy, and although the pain of separation after a long and happy marriage was difficult, as time passed the hurt and loneliness diminished. I became involved in a local church bereavement group to help other people undergoing the effects of the death of a loved one. This enabled me to think of other people's problems without dwelling too much on my own.

John O'Donoghue, an Irish poet, summed it up in the following conclusion to his poem 'Grief':

'More than you, it knows its way and will find the right time to pull and pull
The rope of grief until that hill of tears has reduced to the last drop.
Gradually, you will learn acquaintance with the invisible form of your departed
Having learned to wean your eyes from that gap in the air and be able to enter
The hearth in your soul where your loved one has awaited your return all the
Time. Gradually you will learn acquaintance with the invisible form of your
Departed and when the work of grief is done, the wound of loss will heal'.

Other effects on my life as a widower

My widower status did have an effect on my holidays. In place of two or three weeks, I now restrict holidays to shorter breaks. These are mainly with members of my family and friends. Social occasions such as dinners and dances can be difficult as one stands out as a single person, with consequent constraints. I find this with Rotary events for couples, and now tend to avoid them. However, there are compensations when one is with close friends who are able to mention Maeve's name without embarrassment.

I have learned to be on my own, not with feelings of being a victim but reflecting on the happy occasions with our family through good and some difficult times. I feel grateful that we enjoyed 54 years of married life. As a widower, apart from normal minor pains and aches commensurate with age, I count my blessings and am now more aware how lucky I am to reach what is an advanced age without serious illness. I have learned to accept the inevitability of being on my own. Losing a loved one is the result of age and illnesses. Being of Celtic origin, death is considered a passing from this world to a different world beyond. This was underlined by my wife's funeral service, which was attended by a wide range of family and friends.

We viewed this service as a celebration of her life when we could recall the happier times. All those who attended were invited to a local hotel to continue that celebration in their own way. This supported me and my family, which was greatly appreciated.

I attach a simple graph which shows 'The Experience of Loss/Grief'. The stages shown will vary for each person, but I have felt a number of them. I hope that this account of my wife's passing and the consequences might help others to live with and come to terms with their own grief.

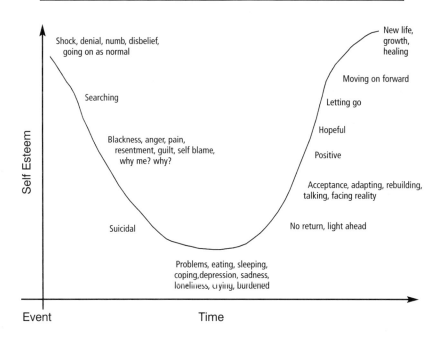

The Experience of Loss/Grief

Shock, denial, numb, disbelief, going on as normal

Searching

Blackness, anger, pain, resentment, guilt, self blame, why me? why?

Suicidal

Problems, eating, sleeping, coping, depression, sadness, loneliness, crying, burdened

No return, light ahead

Acceptance, adapting, rebuilding, talking, facing reality

Positive

Hopeful

Letting go

Moving on forward

New life, growth, healing

Self Esteem

Event

Time

Jimmy Mulhall

The pre-war years

I am very much a product of Durham, born in Langley Moor in July 1919 and going later to the Johnston School where I passed my school certificate in 1935. In those days many could not afford to stay on for higher school certificate and very few went on to university, so in 1936 I became a trainee manager for the City of Durham Gas Company.

Three years later on 3rd September 1939, I was on an International Friendship League holiday in Keswick with male and female teenagers from Germany, France, Holland, Spain and the Baltic states when the Prime Minister announced that we were at war with Germany. Pandemonium invaded our serene walking and climbing holiday when it was also stated that all foreigners had to leave the country within 48 hours or be interned for the duration of the war. Friendships ended, packing took place and arrangements were made immediately to take the majority to London and the rest to Newcastle for travel abroad.

My war years

My war years were tumultuous, and the highlights and lowlights can only be briefly summarised here. Rather than wait for call-up, I volunteered and joined the 3rd Battalion of the Coldstream Guards in October 1939. After a period of intensive training, in March 1940 we sailed in a convoy of 14 ships (minus two that were sunk in the Bay of Biscay), carrying about 3000 troops in dreadful living conditions, for six weeks all the way round Africa to the Suez Canal, where we disembarked.

We then became motorised to cover the huge mileages of the Western Desert where we were heavily involved in battles with the Italians and with the German Afrika Korps, from whom I was lucky to be one of the 200 who escaped capture in Tobruk. We were then part of the Eighth Army which pushed the enemy right across Tripolitania and northwards into Tunisia before they surrendered in the Cap Bon Peninsula.

I remember well 9th September 1943 when we invaded Italy, but in November we were almost pushed back into the sea by the Germans and I became so ill with malaria that I was taken in a well-marked hospital ship to Algiers. Returning to Italy in December, I was shattered to be captured by a German patrol when I was on a reconnaissance mission south of the river at Garigliano before the final attack on Monte Casino. After being interviewed by a German colonel, who spoke perfect English as he was an ex-Oxford graduate, I was taken by railway to Bavaria in appalling insanitary cattle trucks with 60 prisoners per truck. All PoWs interests were different, but I was only interested in escaping, the excitement and fear of which were almost unbearable. We deceived, stole and tunnelled to escape, and between January 1944 and March 1945 I made three escapes, the most successful being largely on my own or with the help of another. Inevitably, the trauma of the war transformed my life unforgettably, but on the plus side I was 'Mentioned in Despatches' three times.

A Durham couple

After my long war service, settling back in Durham was not easy, but on 3rd May 1947 I married Vivienne in St. Margaret's Church, Durham. She was born in Lanchester on 29th September 1928, and at 18 was nine years younger than me. Vivienne had only worked as a trainee secretary, but later she was for many years secretary to the well-known Dean Wild of Durham.

We lived for three years in two rooms in Sutton Street and then four years in a council house on Sunderland Road, where priority was given to returning servicemen. New private housing development commenced only in 1952, a very important date as a new house had an inside toilet, bath, refrigerator etc. and all the neighbours were ex-service people saving for a deposit to purchase a house of their own. My new house cost £2,100, when I believe my weekly wage with the City of Durham Gas Co. was only £5. I like to think and am pleased how lucky I am to have lived within the city boundary for all of my life, apart from during the war.

Vivienne's death

Tuesday 19th December 2000 was a wonderful sunny day. I was pottering and Vivienne was colouring her hair for going on our Christmas holidays with our eldest daughter Julia and her family in South Wales, starting on the Friday. She looked fit and well, and I said "You are dyeing your hair soon", to which she replied "If it doesn't take, I have two days to do it again". After tea, I was washing up in the kitchen while Vivienne and our younger daughter Victoria were watching 'Coronation Street' on television in the sitting room, when at 6.45pm Victoria rushed in to say that her Mum was making an awful noise in her throat. I hurried through to find her still sitting in her chair with her eyes closed. I carried her to the floor, tore off her blouse and bra and administered first aid that I had learnt in the Boy Scouts and in the Army, but there was no reaction. I gave her many, many kisses, but little did I know that those were for her life. Her lips were cold and I was convinced she was dead a matter of 15 minutes from when Victoria had rushed into the kitchen. The paramedic team arrived 20 minutes later, asked us to leave the room, and I could hear their electric equipment being used for about 45 minutes, but to no avail. I was convinced that she died of a severe heart attack, which proved to be true when I consulted the death certificate issued by the doctor at Dryburn Hospital, Durham (at that time paramedics did not have such authority).

Grief and widowhood

My family and I were grief-stricken. We had not had a word from Victoria, it was five days before Christmas, and to make matters worse the crematorium was to be closed until 3rd January 2001. Fortunately, a service was arranged at St. Margaret's Church within two days, which many, many friends attended but I remember little about it except holding Victoria's hand throughout and escaping with her to the cortege to await the others.

Victoria did not understand: "Why, why Dad?" Curiously, she showed no tears at home or in the church. She was silent for many hours, and the scenario did not help her oncoming mental state one bit. Travelling back from South Wales for the cremation on 3rd January, she was completely silent for more than six hours, but went to work at the National Savings the next day.

I did not have any hallucinations, but dreams yes. I had seen many deaths on the battlefield in the Western Desert, Tunisia, Pantellaria and Italy, and many emaciated Russians who did not recognise the Geneva Convention, but then I did not have a Vivienne and was young and cold-blooded. I do not believe in life after death – how could there be? The death of a loved one must be the most traumatic experience anyone has to face. No two people cope with it in the same way; some are angry, some are numb, but I cannot believe that total recovery from one's wife's death is possible.

My house remains the same after ten years – same curtains, carpets, pictures, holiday presents from Whitley Bay, Holy Island etc. – but I have started to give away some of those precious memories. All Vivienne's clothes were taken away to South Wales where Julia disposed of them, and her jewellery of course was divided by the two girls.

Sadness and grief may strike at any time, with tears and misery. I am still overwhelmed with guilt having a second daughter with Vivienne when she was 39 and me 48, especially as Victoria is unlikely to have a full mental recovery. Much of my time is now taken with visits to her in hospital, and talking to other mentally ill patients. Moreover, I have not engaged a solicitor to process the Court of Protection order; doing it myself was a good time filler. I am not envious when I see many older people relying on their family to provide support and care, but sorry that my daughter Julia lives 350 miles away.

The future

The future at 91 years of age is still worth playing for, but fear of personal injury increases. I still cope with my needs adequately, but realise that one day I'll be no longer able to drive, which will be a great blow to convenient shopping.

Yesterday I went to the library to put my name down to read ex-President George Bush's biography, and at the same time picked up a book of quotations, of which the following seem very appropriate regarding old men:

> *"It is sad for a man to attain the age when girls consider him harmless"*.

> "I don't need to be remembered for my age; I have a bladder to do that for me".

> *"How long do you want to wait until you start enjoying life? When you are 65 you get social security, not girls"*.

> "The old believe anything, the middle aged suspect everything, the young know everything" (Oscar Wilde).

> *"First you forget names, then you forget faces, then you forget to pull your zipper up, then you forget to pull your zipper down"*.

John Clarke

My wife's dementia

To all intents and purposes, I became a widower when my dear wife 'Dig' (a nickname) no longer knew me, some eight and a half years before she died on 15 September, 2008. Her vascular multi-infarct dementia had started 18 months earlier, when we had been married for 43 years and she was 65, and since then I had been looking after her at home, but with increasing difficulty. An early sign was when she made tea for three, instead of for the two of us. When I questioned her about it, she explained that she had made one for herself and one each for the two of me! I asked her where the other John was, and she replied that of course there were two of me and I should not be so ludicrous.

Adjustment to my new status was not easy. For the first 43 years of our very happy marriage, my wife and I had enjoyed clearly differentiated life-styles. I was an academic, writing, lecturing and chairing academic committees locally and internationally, while she organised and administered our family and home as well as teaching in primary schools during the early and later years. We both enjoyed and accepted our separate academic and domestic spaces, but supported each other as much as possible. We rarely argued, as on the whole she did not read my books and papers, and I had a more peripheral role in the home and with the family, but occasionally she would attend one of my more public lectures and I was allowed to paint the white walls of the house and to do the gardens. I would also take her to the many local market towns at weekends, where we enjoyed pub lunches before she started her afternoon shopping. The fact that I was partially colour blind meant that she had a much better eye for buying clothes (e.g. all mine), pictures and antiques, and she did so with my ready acceptance while often I browsed through bookshops.

With frequent small strokes, she deteriorated rapidly by steps rather than the more gradual decline experienced by sufferers of

Alzheimer's disease. Soon she had to be watched over all day long, and it took most of my time – a considerable contrast to our previously highly differentiated lives. I had to gently remove her from membership of a school governing body, a hospice council and a prison visitors centre. Having walked out of our house and been lost in the city several times, she was unable to undertake any shopping (although that had been a favourite occupation), and we relied on my minimal catering ability to provide meals at home, or better still in any pub or restaurant within easy distance. Holidays such as cruises were a blessing, but she had to be kept in sight or under lock and key, especially at night-time. Once when we were in a Manchester hotel going on holiday to Madeira, she went to our bedroom toilet and then left the room in her nightdress with the bedroom door locking automatically behind her; I don't know how long it was before I discovered that she was missing from the room, but eventually found her at the other side of the hotel.

One of the most memorable family events was when in 2000 I arranged for us both to go with her sister Ruth to stay for a few days in a hotel near Ashbourne in Derbyshire, her home town where her other sister and some of her family still lived. I invited 72 members of the extended family to an afternoon party, and 62 came! Obviously there were some who couldn't come because of distance and marital break-ups, but the party was a great success. Those attending never stopped talking, including the children who had never met before but enjoyed running around the beautiful garden on a lovely sunny day. Dig was a little overwhelmed by meeting so many of her extended family who she did not recognise, and unfortunately it was the last time that many of us met before her funeral eight years later. When I was busy for a day or two and away from home, her sister Ruth who lived in York (very accessible by train in less than an hour) was extremely helpful in caring for her, especially after the death of her husband, as were a number of her close friends and former teacher colleagues.

As her condition worsened and she could not manage finances, I had to take out enduring power of attorney over her. She was a very private person who did not like mention of the word 'dementia', so I had to look after her mainly by myself at home for two and a half years until January 2001, when carers from the Social Services and the Alzheimer Society began to come in for a few hours a day to assist me. Earlier she had resisted any recourse to such help. Unfortunately, this extra care lasted less than two months, as in late February 2001 she deteriorated so suddenly from a particular TIA (transient ischaemic attack) that she was taken immediately into Chester-le-Street hospital, where it became rapidly evident that she was not going to come home. She remained there for three months of assessment, initially with no medication, wandering around in a daze, unable to control her functions, looking lopsided and completely lost. After a gloomy diagnosis suggesting that she might die within a year, she was moved in May 2001 as one of the first residents into the newly completed St Aidan Lodge care home for the elderly demented in Framwellgate Moor, only two miles away from our home. There she was so well cared for that she remained unexpectedly in her own little mental world, not knowing me or any of her family, for over seven and a quarter years until she died in September 2008.

Living alone before being widowed

So before becoming a widower I was living with my wife but unrecognised by her for at least a year, and then separate from her for more than seven and a quarter years while she was living in the care home. In other words, I was pre-widowed, going to see her every day but not being recognised as her husband. Unlike some of my elderly friends who became widowers very abruptly a few hours after their wives had collapsed terminally ill, I lived alone long before I became a widower, but that merely illustrates the many differences in all our lives.

Now I was in sole charge of the home and of my lifestyle, which involved many new difficulties, particularly financial. In the early days I had been successful in obtaining an 'attendance allowance' for Dig from the Department of Work and Pensions, but it transpired rapidly that I would be responsible for all the costs of her residence in a care home – many hundreds of pounds a week – which would not be accounted for by the NHS. Escalating annually and accounting for roughly half of our combined incomes, that remained the situation until February 2008, seven months before her death, when the NHS decided that I no longer had to pay for her residence at St Aidan Lodge care home because she was so poorly that she required 'continuing care'. It was a subtle variation in definition, but it had a dramatic uplifting effect upon my finances.

Another significant change was that I was not only losing my wife and marriage but also my professional status and identity. I had officially retired from my university post in 1990, from the chairmanship of the Durham Health Authority in 1996 and from the chairmanship of the North East Regional Committee of the National Lottery Charities Board/Community Fund in 2002, and was now in my seventies, and coming closer to my academic 'sell-by-date'. In less demand, I was no longer being invited nationally and internationally to contribute as an editor, author, reviewer, lecturer or assessor. The last of my 97 book reviews was published in 2001, and my last major conference paper was given in 2002. The only real role that I retained was the voluntary chairmanship of the County Durham Foundation's grants committee. Although I continued to write some shorter academic papers and to give lectures to local societies, I was being asked to do much less.

All this required some personal adjustment, but it gave me more time to deal with my varied domestic duties and to discuss with our daughters and lawyers some financial and legal problems, including my will (we could not alter my wife's), a trust should she survive me, and my daughters' enduring power of attorney over me.

Ups and downs

I realise that I drive myself fairly hard and give myself little time to stand and stare, but events tend to take over parts of one's life, and they have their distinct 'ups and downs'. Thus it was in 2003. It started with the announcement of a royal award for me for services to the university, the county and the North-East and later involved a wonderful investiture ceremony at Buckingham Palace, but this was followed in London by the tragic death from a brain tumour of one of my sons-in-law at the early age of 34, leaving my youngest daughter with two little children aged three and one. He had been a very successful investment banker, and the funeral was huge, but it meant that during the following months I paid many visits to my daughter and her children. As she was left in comfortable circumstances, later I helped her to purchase, decorate and furnish a lovely chalet in the French Alps, which over succeeding years has proved a very good investment. Of course, my dear wife knew nothing about all this or anything else, and although it was not the only death amongst our extended family and friends she would have been particularly mortified by this close tragedy.

During the following year I experienced another major 'down'. When I visited the local hospital to have some solar keratoses on my hand removed by burning, it was discovered that I was suffering from a common old men's complaint, prostate cancer, something I needed like a hole in the head. It meant months of treatment, starting with a series of hormone therapy injections to reduce my testosterone, followed six months later by 36 daily radiotherapy treatments. Unfortunately, before these were administered I fell down my garden steps on black ice and badly broke my left elbow, so that I had to be an in-patient for a week in the local hospital where screws, wires and a plate had to be inserted into my left arm, which is now permanently slightly bent. Moreover, as I could not drive for three months I had to be taken by ambulance for the radiotherapy treatments in the Northern Centre for Cancer Treatment in Newcastle. The ambulances ruled my life for seven weeks, as they collected and deposited me at different times of the day.

Being partly out of action, it was not an easy period to be living alone, especially as our golden wedding anniversary fell in the midst of it all on 2nd April 2005, but this great event was lost on my wife so there was no celebration. During this difficult period I became very conscious of how greatly I was assisted by numerous members of the medical, nursing and social services, as well as in many other ways by all my Durham friends. They enabled me to get back to many minor activities to preserve my health and sanity: swimming, walking, gardening, house painting, and attending concerts at the Sage in Gateshead and plays at the Durham Gala Theatre.

Fortunately, despite living quite far from my children and grand-children they all came to see me at various junctures, so that I was never really alone. It was a comfort to return to some semblance of normality, especially a series of family events, as despite their dispersal around the country the family has always played a crucial role in our ageing lives. Late in 2005, there were two delightful family weddings. The first was that of my eldest granddaughter Claire who married a fellow investment banker Simon in Essex, presenting me with three new step great-grandchildren: Georgia, Hannah and Jack. The second wedding was in Hampstead where my widowed youngest daughter Lucy married Tom, a young consultant surgeon of New Zealand origin. I was rather daunted by having to make a speech, standing uncertainly on a chair, before a large number of guests. I welcomed the restoration of some gender balance in my family, saying that I had been married for more than 50 years and my parents for nearly 69 years, having been known to us as the 'Gs and Bs', because they always referred to the good days and bad days – now I know what they meant. Another memorable family highlight was when I was taken by my three daughters and eldest granddaughter for a tightly packed nostalgic weekend in Paris, where I had been a French government post-graduate scholar back in the early 1950s.

Unfortunately, during all this time my wife was completely demented, knowing nothing at all. Yet, as there is no batting order, many of my old friends died before her, although they had long been fitter than her; for example, four close friends died in the last four months of 2006. Sadly, I was asked to speak at several funerals – not an easy task, and I much prefer to speak at 80th birthday parties. In general, however, my life became increasingly filled with more or less routine events: *daily* visits to my wife, feeding myself, housework and gardening; *weekday* swimming; *weekend* walks when the weather was fine; *weekly* club lunches: *fortnightly* 'grumpy old men's' lunches; *monthly* club dinners and U3A meetings; *intermittent* concerts, plays, funerals, birthday parties and university lectures; and *six-monthly* check-ups with the oncologist.

In March 2008, seven years after my wife went into hospital, it was decided that she should go into 'continuing care', because she could do nothing except breathe and swallow, and of course she was not expected to live for a long time. It was another sad stage in her continuous decline, and her forthcoming passing blighted the summer. However, life is all about highs and lows, and in marked contrast our youngest daughter gave birth to her third child, who became our sixth grandchild and third grandson and who I was delighted and flattered to learn was to be given my Christian name.

In September 2008, Dig spent the last eight days of her life in hospital, mostly fast asleep, but when I went into see her on Monday 15th she looked at me unusually wide-eyed, so I kissed her and told her that I loved her and then almost as if she had waited for me to come she closed her eyes and died, almost precisely at midday. Although overwhelmed by her death, I felt that the end of her terrible illness was a blessing for her, because she was such a private person who would have hated her predicament. It was also the end of a wonderful marriage that had lasted more than 53 years and about which I never had any regrets, except for the last ten long years when we were separated by her dementia. They were so exhausting and demanding. I never wanted her to die, and yet for years she had no life worth living. The new millennium had been a very painful time for us.

The initial aftermath

The initial aftermath following my wife's death was overtaken by writing numerous letters in response to condolences and kindnesses of our many friends. And of course all my family played important roles at the funeral, which took place on Saturday 20th September, with a service at St. Margaret's Church, followed by the burial in Bow Cemetery and a large tea reception for friends and family at Collingwood College. The whole day was so overwhelming, an event for which one is never prepared.

There were also the legal necessities associated with her will, but they did not seem very complicated because I had had power of attorney over her affairs for many years, and her finances had been simplified. Her will had to remain unchanged during her long illness, and it left everything to me.

As we had been expecting her to die for many years, the immediate shock did not last, and in a few weeks I was back to my autumnal way of life: sweeping leaves, picking and stewing apples and pears, tidying up the garden, having a flu' jab, visiting my daughters and friends, and keeping as busy as possible. On the other hand, as I was approaching 80 years of age my activities had tapered off considerably, a fact faced by most of the elderly. Nevertheless, in January 2009 less than four months after the death of my wife, I had a wonderful 80th birthday party in Trevelyan College attended by about 80 guests. Organised by my daughters, it involved not only many of the extended family but numerous Durham friends, a barber-shop quartet, a magnificent birthday cake topped by the title of my best-known book, and five lovely little speeches by five of my six grandchildren (not the one-year old!). Everyone was so kind and supportive. I only wish that my wife could have been there, but it seemed to end the immediate aftermath of her death.

Widowed

Now in my eighties, I am several years above the rising average male life expectancy in Britain. Older men are living much longer, especially those of us who have worked in the service sector with 'clean' jobs. Of course, one has to recognise that one has experienced the great majority of one's life, which seems to pass at an ever-increasing rate, so that one has to live for the present and make the best of all opportunities.

My life now is very different from what it was in the past, contracting in many ways but expanding in others. Then it was dominated by marriage, the family and my academic work. Now I live alone, have no family living nearer than fifty miles, have all the usual domestic chores, take few holidays, have no travel-to-work or academic functions, and even service within the voluntary sector has diminished markedly. Fortunately, the small city of Durham offers innumerable social possibilities of clubs, societies, friendships and contacts which take up much of one's spare time. One can hardly walk through the city without meeting someone one knows.

Moreover, one can still read and write (or more realistically use the computer), so there is not a lot of spare time.

The future

The future is so uncertain in every conceivable way that no wonder most predictions prove to be fallacious. Certainly, I had no ideas about living alone in my eighties, and yet that is now the reality, and I have no real idea of how long I will live, where or how. Yet I have now come to realise that many of us elderly men living alone have the opportunity of a new life, a new partnership or companionship, even a new home, something perhaps we would not have considered before being widowed. Many of us who have lived alone for a long time in our old age have established a new pattern of life, making new friends and relationships. A new marriage may pose too many problems, not least because of legal complications. After a long marriage, even a new relationship requires courage and energy for which there is no blueprint. It is an act of pioneering for the participants, but with perseverance, mutual compassion and good fortune it may prove to be a wonderful antidote to the loneliness and constraints of old age.

Michael Hill

Abrupt death

Life was good. We had almost eleven years of retirement together, and were looking forward to many more. This idyll was shattered in a matter of five hours, when my wife suffered a massive aneurism. She said that she didn't feel well at 11.00 a.m. and by 4.00 p.m. she had gone – a bolt out of the blue. The frightening thing was that there was no prior warning. Nothing prepares you for this, and your whole world falls apart. We had been childhood sweethearts and married for 48 years.

Reaction

It is almost four years since she died, and her loss is still felt. The grief lingers, but life has to go on. I suppose that I am lucky in that we have always belonged and been involved with the church wherever we have lived, and this has given me great comfort and support. For the first two or three months you wander around existing rather than living, but with the help of family and very good friends a new phase of your life begins. Going back into society on your own for the first time can be a bit daunting as people with the best intentions in the world commiserate on your loss and this brings the memories flooding back. Fortunately, this period soon passes and you start living again, without being reminded of your loss.

Adjustment

My career was such that I had led a very independent life, and this has helped me to adjust to living on my own. It is not until you are on your own that you appreciate and recall how much your wife did, and that it now devolves on you. Shopping for groceries and everyday things was a chore to begin with and required many extra trips for forgotten/necessary things. You soon realise that you have to write things down in order to avoid unnecessary journeys.

Having to cook for oneself is another skill one has to master, and I must admit that I find this quite satisfying. I won't say that I eat as healthily as I should, but I do indulge myself and eat what I want to!

Friends

I think that we were lucky in that we have a large number of friends of very long standing, 40 years or more, and these are the mainstay of my new life along with the clubs and societies I belong to including Rotary, Probus and U3A. If you are willing to participate in these societies, you can live a very busy and full life, and this has been the case for me.

On the other hand, I find that the thought of going on holiday on my own does not appeal, it leaves me cold. Apart from the fact that my career involved travelling the world, the idea of sitting in a restaurant on my own is not very appealing, and to intrude on other people's holidays is an imposition which is not for me. I am sure that there are many holidays one could take, but for the moment, I am quite content to stay at home.

There is a life after the death of your partner, but you have to find it. It will not find you unless you are willing to participate and be part of society again. Life does go on. I like the following poem by David Harkins:

You can shed tears that she is gone
Or you can smile because she has lived.
You can close your eyes and pray that she will come back
Or you can open your eyes and see all that she has left.
Your heart can be empty because you cannot see her
Or you can be full of the love which you shared.
You can turn your back on tomorrow and live yesterday
Or you can be happy for tomorrow because of yesterday.
You can remember her and only that she has gone
Or you can cherish her memory and let it live on.
You can cry and close your mind, be empty and turn your back
Or you can do what she would want: smile, open your eyes love
and live on.

Pat Woodward

Widowhood

I have now been on my own for four years, but my situation, although not unique, is unusual in that my late wife was my senior by seven and a half years. This meant that in our early married life (we married in 1951) Helen and I were about even in terms of life expectancy, as at that time women on average outlived men by seven years. This gap has closed a little in recent years, but as we had both survived service during the Second World War, and had thus seen much death and destruction, it was an irrelevant statistic. We were always prepared for either of us to go first, but the real sadness was that our last years together were blighted by her dementia from Alzheimer's disease. Her departure after 55 years of a happy marriage, although a sad parting, was in the natural order of things, and whilst I miss her I entered widowhood without much difficulty.

Domesticity

Luckily I have always been a well domesticated man, and with the help of the family was able to keep Helen at home and look after her almost to the end. My father died young at 47, and during his later years was a very sick man having suffered privation and serious illness as a prisoner-of-war for over four years after being captured at Mons in August 1914. He was never the same again after release from the army, and had continuous bouts of illness which needed home nursing. There was no NHS then and all doctors' bills had to be paid, so my mother expected her four children from an early age to give her what help they could with domestic chores, and I soon found myself able to make a bed, wash dishes and even do a bit of cooking.

This early domestic training was enhanced at my school, the Duke of York's Royal Military at Dover, and similar self-sufficiency later in the Royal Air Force left me highly qualified in all branches of house-work, particularly now that there are so many appliances to ease the workload. Thus I have no difficulty in being able to look after myself on my own, but am very well aware that this is not the case for many men in similar circumstances. If family members live close by some help may be expected, but courses in domestic work, including cooking, are readily available these days and should be used by men without embarrassment. If nothing else, it gets one out of the house and introduces new faces.

Costs

Widowhood can make a big difference economically, but this is a subjective matter and very few cases will be similar. It depends on many factors, predominantly financial, which can have a big effect especially where one's wife's pension income ceases. My experience is that costs generally remain the same, with perhaps small reductions here and there, and it is certainly not true that losing a partner halves the costs. For instance, the single person discount for council tax is only 25%.

Social life

From the social aspect, widowhood brings an abrupt end to some activities, not only during the period of mourning, as couples are much easier to entertain than a man on his own. For women it can be worse, but nothing like the extreme length of purdah suffered by ladies when I was young. As I am fond of company and gregarious, I have many friends who with my family, though widely spread, keep well in touch and ensure that boredom is rare. Short-term good company can also be found in the well run pubs and clubs, of which there are several in Durham. Also clubs and societies can be useful in widening one's circle of friends, but personally I have never been a club man.

Holidays for singles are a problem due to the high premium charged if one doesn't share accommodation. I try to visit friends and relatives to avoid this 'tax' on singles, and up to now I have been made very welcome. I have just returned from a short cruise for which the single premium was not too bad. I enjoyed myself but did a lot of talking, probably a release from the silence of a widower's house. I do hope that I am not becoming a bore – another problem of being without a wife to tell one to 'shut up'.

Philip Tattersall

Marriage

Mavis and I met while we were undergraduates, I in my second year and Mavis in her first. The occasion was a party to which I had been initially reluctant to go, but subsequent events showed how right was the decision to attend. We were married some four years later when I graduated, and were married for nearly 46 years before her death after a painful illness lasting six months. That was nine years ago, and so my experience of widowhood is much shorter than that of marriage.

We were lucky to spend six years together after I retired. A very significant decision was made at just about the time of my retirement – to stay in Durham rather than move away. We made that decision based on the friends we had made in the 35 years we had lived in Durham, and on the accessibility of hospitals, the theatre and concert facilities. Subsequent events have shown the validity of that choice.

Domesticity and family

During my retirement I had gradually taken over more cooking, and during Mavis's illness and time in hospital this interest and ability became an essential tool, an interest that has continued and flourished, enabling me to entertain at home and repay the hospitality that many kind friends have shown. This continuing relationship with others is, to my mind, an important aspect in coping with the changes that bereavement has brought.

My family has been and continue to be a tremendous support, but they live away from the North East so a measure of self-sufficiency has been important. Companionship at home was at first given by

Tom and Violetta, the last in a line of Siamese cats, but who died some six months after Mavis. I then had six months without a pet. A friend remarked that she thought that I was "missing something breathing" when I came into the house, so acting on her advice Smokey came and has fulfilled that role to perfection, or as she would say 'purrfection'. She is both a companion and a dependant, and this aspect of having another living being who needs you is important when you live alone. The question of other permanent relationships has not arisen, and nor have I felt the need or the desire. I somewhat doubt if I have the stamina to undertake such an enterprise now.

Friends, activities and health

I mentioned friends earlier and they are very important, both close friends and acquaintances. Soon after Mavis's death one friend and I started to have lunch together on a regular basis, and from that has grown a group of six similarly placed friends who have fortnightly lunches. We are a diverse group in age and experience, and our discussions are wide ranging. We have sampled the food at a variety of establishments in the area, and travelling to these places shows the beauty and diversity of the region in which we live.

Mental stimulation at home comes from reading, listening to music, crosswords and sudoku, and outside from the U3A, History of Art classes, concerts and the theatre; thank goodness for the Sage, the Gala and the Theatre Royal.

Some 16 years ago I was diagnosed with a progressive neurological condition. At the time I was told "there is nothing we can do about it, it will get worse, but the good news is that it won't kill you". Progression has occurred, and walking long distances is now impossible. However, swimming and regular shorter walks in the Botanical Gardens are good alternatives and through this I have met another group of friends. It is interesting that patterns of friendship change when one is no longer one of a couple; some fade away, others are reinforced, and totally new ones forged.

I still live in the family home that has been mine for some 36 years, too big for one elderly man and his cat but ideal when the family return and for entertaining. This is only possible because of excellent help in home and garden from Joan and George.

Charitable work

Another activity that has become an important part of my life is the chairmanship of the local supporters group of a charity which was very important to Mavis, and I am enjoying my deeper involvement with its activities both personally and because I knew how much it would have meant to her. The role came about on the retirement of the previous chairman and the reluctance of others to take up the post. This not entirely voluntary decision has, in fact, been a blessing in disguise, bringing me into contact with a new circle of acquaintances both locally and nationally, making me look for ways to raise funds and awareness of the charity's work.

Holidays

As a married couple, holidays were in later years taken in Wales or abroad, but widowhood led to a resolution to holiday in the UK. However, an advertisement for a cruise to South America led to a change of heart, and I have discovered the delights that cruise holidays have to offer as a means of seeing the world and also meeting other people. These holidays have usually been taken in the company of my sister and/or friends. My daughter and I continue to visit Wales regularly, a place we love and Mavis's childhood home, thus keeping up a connection going back many years.

The future

Reaching 80 years of age, mortality and the existence of an afterlife are perhaps more pertinent than heretofore. Recently I looked at John Clare's poem 'The Instinct of Hope', and the following relevant lines:

'Is there another world for this frail dust to warm with life and be itself again';

and

'Time wandering onwards keeps its usual pace as seeming anxious of eternity, to meet the calm and find a resting place'.

I have no religious belief, and think that our life in this world should be lived to the full while respecting the lives and beliefs of others. To me where we are going is not to another world, but to ashes and dust, our legacy being what we have done in the world and the family we leave behind. If one phrase sums up the philosophy of this elderly widower living alone, it is 'Live for the day'.

Tony Booth

Family origins

I always take great pride in that I was born in Wigan. My parents had married in 1921, and I was their first and only surviving child, born in 1930, "a pillar on which the whole world stands" or so I was told by one of my Jesuit teachers when I replied to a question of how many brothers and sisters did I have. Mother was from an old Wigan recusant Catholic family, while father's family was in the Church of England. Mother had qualified as a schoolteacher in 1912 and taught until her marriage, when under the rule of the day she had to retire, a rule that was only rescinded in 1940 when she was called back to teaching.

I often think that we 80-year olds are one of the luckier generations. We were brought up in the depression of the early 1930s and saw real poverty. After the war, we had the benefits of a National Health Service, full employment, better pension schemes and a fairer more liberal society to live in. Because of my father's work, we lived until 1936 near the Wigan Athletic football ground where there were many unemployed. Friends of my age were frequently invited to Sunday dinner in my home, and only later did I realise that this was to ensure that they got a good meal.

Schools

In 1936, we moved to a more up-market area of Wigan, where my father insisted that I should go to a local elementary school and not the convent. I was not a particularly good student or well behaved, and after unfortunately crashing my bicycle into our doctor's car I was packed off to a prep school at Freshfield. There I had five happy and interesting years although the Lancashire hotpot on Thursdays was dreadful, and to get a friend to eat the potatoes cost one penny, a third of my weekly pocket money.

The war changed life as schoolmasters left to join the army, and my father who was on the Reserve of Officers was recalled. Our home was rented out, and my mother and I went to live with my grandmother for the duration of the war. In 1943 I took the common entrance exam and moved to Stonyhurst College, where I had four and a half very happy and active years. I had a vision of becoming a vet, but realising that I would not get a place at a veterinary college until after I had completed my national service I chose to go for a career in the army and to go to RMA Sandhurst – to the disappointment of my parents.

The Army

As I was to join the army in April 1948, I left school at the end of the Christmas term in December 1947. After the Christmas holidays I was sent to a local commercial college to learn typing and book-keeping; skills I found useful in later life. In April I reported to a Royal Armoured Corps Training Unit at Barford Camp, Barnard Castle where I was put into a potential officer squad, did a little drill, took amazing initiative tests, and learned to drive 15cwt trucks and Daimler armoured cars.

In August 1948 I entered the RMA Sandhurst where during 18 happy months I made a number of lifelong friends. My experience is that the friends you made at school, Sandhurst and with fellow junior officers in your regiment become close friends. Later in life, whether they had become generals, politicians, successful citizens or had led very quiet lives, you still have greater affinity with them and those you stood in danger with than many of your other normal friends and acquaintances.

On leaving Sandhurst, I was commissioned into my father's old regiment, and joined it in Trieste in January 1950. During my enjoy-able army career, I was stationed in Italy, Germany, Korea, Kenya, Uganda, Southern Cameroons, Zambia, Cyprus, Singapore and of course at various times in Britain and Northern Ireland; serving at both regimental duty and as a staff officer, and meeting interesting people like Kenneth Kaunda and Idi Amin.

Marriage

It was in East Africa that I met my wife. At the end of the emergency, my battalion of the King's African Rifles had moved down to Langata Camp Nairobi and in May 1957 we had a cocktail party. I was introduced to a young girl and after talking to her I invited her to come and watch me play rugby. She had agreed but when she got back to her flat in Nairobi had second thoughts. Fortunately for me her mother was visiting her and told her that not to turn up would be the height of rudeness, and that she should go and leave after the match. She came and stayed, and eighteen months later we were married.

I applied and was selected for voluntary redundancy and left the army in October 1978 to become Assistant Secretary of The North of England Territorial, Auxiliary and Volunteer Reserve Association and moved to County Durham. We had had twenty years of army married life and lived in no less than 13 different houses in seven countries. My son had attended three schools and my daughters six – today I find it difficult to understand how politicians can consider taking away the benefit of educational allowance from service families.

Civilian life

I had no regrets in leaving the army, which had been an enjoyable chapter of life, with the benefits of comradeship and loyalty. Of course, living in an authoritarian society has its drawbacks. Blame cannot be laid on anybody, but scapegoats are found. There can be no questioning of decisions. Perhaps I was always cynical, and realised that whilst you must admire individuals for their abilities you don't necessarily have to respect them. I had seen corruption during my time in Africa, so the recent behaviour of parliamentarians came as no surprise to me, as it is now becoming more open in our society, and corrupt persons will no longer be protected by a code of secrecy. It has been confirmed what I had always been told as a youngster when I complained that something was not fair: 'we do not live in a fair world'.

My civilian employment introduced me to a new world. I met people from all walks of society and people with a variety of jobs and views. Through my wife and daughters' interest in horses, we became involved with horse driving trials. Initially I groomed or (as I prefer to call it) was the navigator for my youngest daughter. Sadly in 1988 I was sacked, not for being unfit or too heavy but because I held my breath or made an exclamation at the more hair-raising moments of an obstacle. Then I became and remain a steward, and served as a health and safety officer until I was 70.

Widowhood and friends

Tragedy struck the family in 1994 when my wife was found to have acute myeloid leukaemia, and sadly after six months of treatment she died in September of that year. Fortunately, although due to retire in January, I was permitted to carry on working for an extra 18 months and was later taken on as a part-time consultant. I became involved with various charities, joining the Soldiers, Sailors, Airmen & Families Association (SSAFA), first as a caseworker and then became the County Branch Secretary, a post retained until my retirement from full-time employment when I became a Divisional Treasurer, which I still occupy at 80. Also I became a caseworker for the Officers Association, and still undertake visits when called upon. Invited to volunteer to be a trustee and committee member of the Durham Community Alarm Trust, I was for some eight years chairman and later deputy chairman until it closed in 2008. All these voluntary roles, though not onerous, kept me occupied and allowed me to repay something back to society.

At a lunch party about a year after my wife had died, I met a family friend who had earlier been a member of the County Durham SSAFA centenary fund-raising committee, and had also been recently widowed. With similar interests, we became good friends and started going out together. The big snag with old age and widowhood is that going out by oneself is very lonely. A companion, male or female, is to be recommended. Sadly in 2005 my friend's health started to fail, and in 2008 she had a major stroke and had to move into a nursing home. Then it was decided that she should be moved to the Midlands to be nearer her sons and their families, and so until her death in September 2010 I visited her every month.

Fortunately my loneliness was reduced again, this time by an invitation to join the *'Grumpy Old Men'*, a gathering of six like-minded men who meet once a fortnight for lunch. It might possibly be said that we are politically incorrect in today's world. However, our rules are based on experience which comes with age! We keep to six because when you go out to a pub you can always get a table for six, and you are more likely to have one conversation. Ours must be interesting, as we are often aware that others nearby are listening in, nodding their heads in agreement or smiling with a satisfied look on their faces!

Truisms

● Age has taught us that there are two sides to every argument, which is right or which is wrong is anybody's opinion, as there are two sides to every coin. Inevitably we are right!

● Global warming is a matter of opinion and not for us the end of civilisation. It too has happened before and the world has not come to an end.

● Friendship is more important than love; long-term friendships can grow into love, though as you get older love becomes more a matter of caring than the younger generation's idea of a loving relationship.

● We oldies have learnt that most things are a matter of opinion. You cannot believe everything you read in the papers, but with the experience of age on your side you know that you are incredibly wise and are probably always right.

● Watching television is insufficient to keep your mind active. Oldies are strongly advised to read books or at least a newspaper daily. Newspapers also give you the advantage of exercising your brain with crosswords, sudoku or both if you are good at both words and logic.

- Membership of a church or local community organisation can be very rewarding. They both provide a feeling of belonging and can often give comfort and advice to older members of society when it is most needed.

- Should something annoy you enough to write a letter of objection, by all means write it but don't post it while you are still annoyed. Keep it overnight, and the next day read it and decide whether it should be toned down before posting. We tend to express ourselves very badly when we are angry or annoyed.

- Widowhood initially leaves us with a feeling of grief or shock. Fortunately, for most of us time is a great healer. However, you will inevitably feel a pang of pain when on your travels you pass a place you and your spouse used to visit. Take comfort and consolation that the pang is reminding you of the happy times you had together in the past. You have not forgotten your loved one, nor should you ever.

Advice

Very elderly men on the whole are unprepared for widowhood. Girls were on marriage expected to give up their jobs and became responsible for looking after their husband, children and the family home. Men were supposedly the breadwinners and took little if any role in the household, apart from paying the bills! The only things most of us had knowledge of were cleaning shoes, pressing shirts and trousers, cleaning grates and laying fires. Most of us had no culinary skills, apart from mess-tin cooking. Our few skills were mostly acquired in the armed forces during the war or national service. Widowhood or a sick spouse opens up a new world. You have to start being responsible for the household chores, but don't despair, necessity is the mother of invention, and it is surprising how quickly we learn household cleaning skills. Modern cookbooks are easy to follow; they tell you everything apart from how to cook vegetables, which you have to learn by trial and error. However, until experience is gained, most men need a timer.

Advice to all when they retire, if they are in good health, is to keep busy both mentally and physically. Age does not diminish your intelligence, but you take longer to do things and can at times be forgetful, particularly remembering names. Don't worry if at times when you go upstairs you have to come down to remember what you went up for. This happens to everyone sooner or later. Try to remember you have a great advantage over the younger generations in that you have experience, and so much which is thought to be new is in fact old hat. It has all been done before.

Should you or your spouse become frail, don't allow pride to stop you from seeking help. Your local health authorities and social services are there to help when it is needed. Also charities such as the citizens advice bureaux and Age UK/Elderly Benefits (formerly Age Concern and Help the Aged) will advise and if necessary help individuals to apply for any benefits they might be entitled to, such as disabled car parking permits and attendance allowances. Provided you have a 'need' rather than a 'want', charities will be very helpful with their advice.

Finally, I would advise older persons not to say 'I think I must be getting old', certainly not in front of their sons or daughters, for inevitably you will hear them reply 'Getting? – You are old!'

CONCLUSION

The varied stories of the elderly widowers living alone who have contributed to this collection might have been supplemented by many more, had we searched the local highways and byways. A mammoth volume could then have been assembled, because any population comprises an immense diversity of individuals with very different tales to tell. Of course for purposes of understanding some of the contributors might have been grouped into contrasting social or economic classes or even political parties, but personal differences often cannot be easily categorised. People do not fall readily into lots.

Nevertheless, there is no doubt that in Britain there are more and more elderly widowers living alone who have survived unexpectedly longer than their wives, who were generally younger. They have become a small but noteworthy section of the population, for whom it has been an enjoyable exercise to offer some of them an opportunity to express themselves. With very long pasts in common, undoubtedly they differ from other groups of people and many have distinctive ideas and points of view, despite the fact that today's much younger politicians and more fashionable social leaders often ignore and neglect them.

Our early years

As all our authors are aged 75 or more, they were all born long before the Second World War, and many of them can recall those pre-war years. The older ones above their early eighties served within that war, a fact which meant harrowing experiences, prolonged absences from home, and profound effects upon all aspects of their lives. Moreover, all the slightly less old members of our group in their late seventies and early eighties remember well those war years. They often served in cadet forces, witnessed the importance of all the voluntary services, such as the Home Guard and the ARP, and after the war nearly all were conscripted or volunteered at some time or other for two years of military service, as until 1960 it was compulsory for all medically fit men unless otherwise excused.

Consequently, our experiences as young adult men were quite different from those of today. Unless given special concession, every man had to join one of the armed forces in his late teenage or early adult years, and was introduced to military discipline. In addition, society in general was much more disciplined during the deprivation and rationing of the war and early post-war years. So everyone experienced the accompanying constraints, shortages and hardships of one sort or another, and all have known a more regimented and hierarchical society where 'service before self' were the watchwords. You did what your seniors told you, in quite sharp contrast with today's much greater stress on self and on personal rights.

We also date from a period when male and female roles in the economy, society and politically were much more distinct than they are nowadays; when health was more precarious and the National Health Service had not been created; when teenagers left school much younger, started work earlier and far fewer went to university; when the mining and manufacturing sectors of the economy were much more significant than nowadays and not so dwarfed by the service sector; and when the political map of the world also differed greatly, with vast parts under British colonial rule so that many Britons sought employment or service within the Empire, although far fewer travelled the world except during wars. In those days holidays abroad were only for the rich, and nobody spoke about globalisation.

So in many ways we were trained to be active and survive adversity; the personal stories show this very clearly. We elderly widowers have not collapsed under the inevitable strains, loneliness and boredom of finding ourselves living alone, of becoming 'a single person household'.

Widowhood

Most of the widowers writing here had long married lives, often exceeding fifty years. Their immediate experiences of widowhood have been very varied. Several wives died abruptly and unexpectedly within a few minutes or hours, without any obvious signs of previous illness; others were ailing for many years, even more than a decade, during much of which they did not know their husbands and even turned against them. Moreover some men were widowed this year; some many years ago. Inevitably, the impact upon husbands of such contrasting deaths differs greatly from very sudden shock to near relief that the agony of seeing one's wife deteriorate over many years is now over. So their grief has varied enormously.

The nature and period of adjustment to male widowhood ('widowerhood') has also varied greatly. Some of us had no time to adjust; others had years. None found it easy, particularly because they are all of a generation who depended on wives to look after much of the domestic side of their family lives. The sudden widowhood of some husbands posed real problems for those who hadn't been much involved in running the home, such as cooking meals, cleaning and entertaining, and who live far away from their children. In contrast the slow death of other wives gave their husbands some time and opportunity for adjustment to their changed situation. And of course some widowers are much more capable of independence, adaptation and hospitality than others. On the whole, our group drive themselves to live very positive lives. For better or worse, we tend to cope with the problems thrust upon us.

Another striking feature of this group of elderly widowers is that they have almost all stayed in their family homes. Unlike many others who have moved to be near family or friends, most have preferred to keep their homes more or less unchanged, partly because they were mainly furnished by their wives, partly because of the problems of creating a new home, and partly because of the extensive social network of their Durham surrounds: neighbours, friends, former colleagues, churches, clubs, pubs, colleges, societies and a physical and social environment which they know and love. Dismantling one's home and starting afresh elsewhere is a daunting prospect for many elderly widowers, as other challenges of aging are numerous such as deteriorating health, the isolation and loneliness felt when family, friends and neighbours either die or move away, and the hazards of severe winters.

Holidays are a problem, as they can never repeat the past. Some don't take them; some take them with their extended families or with friends. Many also prefer to have them in the UK or perhaps take a cruise; one even lectures on cruises.

On the other hand, there are many solaces and comforts that can assist the elderly living alone. Many enjoy living things such as their pet cats, dogs or other animals, along with their gardens, plants and flowers. Most also enjoy good food and wine in pleasant company. Certainly some of our senses deteriorate with age, but the sense of touch remains and is greatly enjoyed; unfortunately the human isolation usually associated with widowhood generally but not always precludes its satisfaction. Moreover, many do not want to take the risks that accompany a new relationship, but as time passes the possibilities sometimes increase and some widowers are very happy to start a new venture with a female friend which transforms their lonely lives, especially when they live far away from their children and grandchildren, who tend to become increasingly important to them.

A positive experience

Meeting together to discuss this project, we felt that we did not want to create a formal organisation, partly because its composition would change too often. However the preparation of this booklet has been a very positive experience for all of us. We have extended our friendships and hospitality and enjoy our meetings chatting about events past and present, and hope that many other elderly widowers will find our reflections and experiences of value and influence, although we are conscious that we do not have all the answers. Generations vary so greatly in their experiences. Perhaps our stories might stimulate a comparable collection written by elderly widows, who would certainly have very different ones to tell, not only because they greatly outnumber elderly widowers.